MARCO POLO



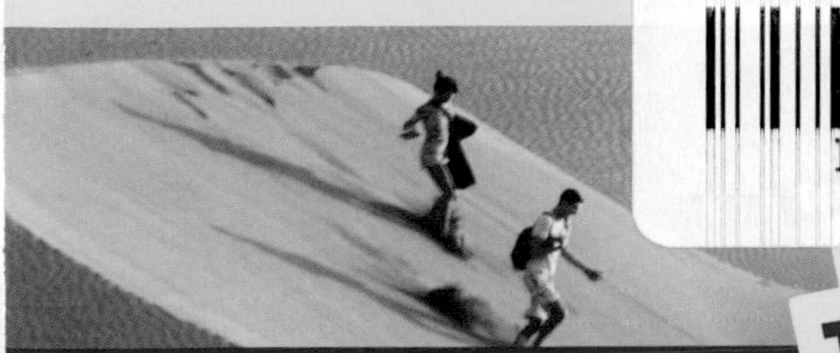

Insider Tips

# GRAN CANARIA

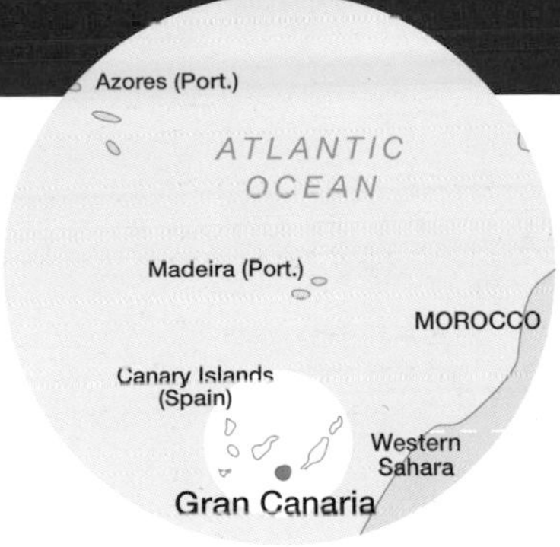
Azores (Port.)
ATLANTIC
OCEAN
Madeira (Port.)
MOROCCO
Canary Islands
(Spain)
Western
Sahara
Gran Canaria

www.marco-polo.com

## SYMBOLS

INSIDER TIP    Insider Tip

★              Highlight

●●●●           Best of ...

☼              Scenic view

☺ Responsible travel: fair
trade principles and the
environment respected

## PRICE CATEGORIES HOTELS

| | |
|---|---|
| *Expensive* | over 150 euros |
| *Moderate* | 70–150 euros |
| *Budget* | under 70 euros |

The prices are for two people
in a double room with
breakfast (hotels) or without
(guesthouses) or for a self-
catering holiday flat

## PRICE CATEGORIES RESTAURANTS

| | |
|---|---|
| *Expensive* | over 20 euros |
| *Moderate* | 10–20 euros |
| *Budget* | under 10 euros |

The prices are for a standard
meal without drinks

On the cover: Beautiful Tejeda between hills and gorges p. 54 | The beaches at Güigüí p. 90

# CONTENTS

The North → p. 58

The South → p. 74

Trips & Tours → p. 96

Road atlas → p. 120

## DID YOU KNOW?

## MAPS IN THE GUIDEBOOK

(128 A1) Page numbers
and coordinates refer to
the road atlas
(0) Site/address located off
the map. Coordinates are
also given for places that are
not marked on the road atlas
Maps of Las Palmas,
Maspalomas, Playa del Inglés
and San Agustín can be found
inside the back cover

**INSIDE BACK COVER:
PULL-OUT MAP →**

## PULL-OUT MAP 𝕄

(𝕄 A–B 2–3) Refers to the
removable pull-out map

# The best MARCO POLO Insider Tips

## Our top 15 Insider Tips

**INSIDER TIP** **Pure wine**

You can purchase unpretentious, organic wines in the Bodega San Juan in El Monte → **p. 67**

**INSIDER TIP** **Just a pile of stones?**

Archaeologists discovered more than 700 ancient Canarian graves in a field of rubble. Find out about the rituals of the original islanders in the *Parque Arqueológico* in Artenara → **p. 88**

**INSIDER TIP** **Local arts and crafts**

FEDAC in Las Palmas sells traditional as well as trendy articles: material with bright-and-breezy designs and lava jewellery (photo right) → **p. 40**

**INSIDER TIP** **A journey back in time**

A walk through the historic district of Telde in *San Francisco* will take you down cobbled streets, past palm trees and whitewashed houses from 1550 → **p. 70**

**INSIDER TIP** **For the sweet-toothed**

Chocolates, delicate macaroons and calorie-rich cakes: the *Dulcería del Nublo* in Tejeda specialises in all things sweet made of almonds → **p. 55**

**INSIDER TIP** **Little Havana**

Salsa, son and samba are really popular in the capital. You can start swaying to the rhythm in *Pequeña Habana* – especially after midnight at weekends → **p. 43**

**INSIDER TIP** **Sleep like a lord**

A sweeping panoramic view over the Valle de Agaete can be enjoyed from the *Finca Las Longueras*, a country house hotel full of character with plush reception rooms and terraces and the scent of orange blossom in the air (photo above) → **p. 65**

**INSIDER TIP** **Dining with donkeys**

Youngsters will be especially attracted by the well cared-for donkeys and children's zoo at the donkey finca *Burro Safari Las Tirajanas*. And grown-ups will like the traditional food – as almost everything is homemade → **p. 97**

# BEST OF ...

**FOR FREE**

● **Free ticket to the art scene**
Experimental, provocative and way-out art free of charge. The *CAAM* in Las Palmas showcases the latest artistic trends from Europe, Africa and America → p. 35

● **Cultural look across the sea**
How about a virtual visit to the neighbouring continent? African artists show their painted, filmed and sound creations in the *Casa África* in Las Palmas – a really exotic day out → p. 35

● **Uplifting experience**
You can witness fervent Spanish religiosity during mass in Las Palmas' *Catedral de Santa Ana*. There is one drawback: entrance is free during church services but you will not be allowed to take photographs → p. 41

● **New Worlds**
Discover America in palatial *Columbus House (Casa de Colón)* in Las Palmas. In those days, the capital of Gran Canaria was just a little unimportant settlement – a scale model shows the city in colonial days → p. 36

● **Taste the rum**
Your tour of the *Arehucas* distillery in Arucas, Europe's largest producer of rum, will take you past giant steel tanks and oak barrels. And you can also taste the excellent rum and liqueurs → p. 60

● **The Virgin in the rock**
The main attraction of the *Virgen de la Cuevita* Chapel in Artenara is its artistic craftsmanship. The whole chapel has been carved out of a cave's rock face (photo) → p. 47

● **Strolling through a Garden of Eden**
You have to pay admission to the Marquise's Garden, the *Jardín del la Marquesa*, in Arucas if you want to see plants from all over the world; however, entrance to the Parque Municipal is free and it also has a wonderful collection of exotic flora → p. 61

●●●● Dots in guidebook refer to 'Best of ...' tips

# ONLY IN GRAN CANARIA
## Unique experiences

● *Fun in a labyrinth of caves*
Have you ever had tapas and wine in a cave? Labyrinth-like
hostelries have been cut into the rock in the *Barranco
de Guayadeque* – keeping up an old tradition as
*Canarios* have always lived in caves (photo) → p. 77

● *See the island in the sun from 'Snow Peak'*
The name of Gran Canaria's highest mountain,
*Pico de las Nieves*, means 'Snow Peak' although
it is very rarely covered in white. However, the
view of the steep precipices and gorges, high
plateaus and needle-like pinnacles is always an
unforgettable experience → p. 49

● *Flowery cheese*
'Flower cheese', *queso de flor*, is the most unusual Canarian
dairy product. It tastes especially good accompanied by a
glass of red wine in the *Bar El 7* in Santa María de Guía → p. 68

● *Reservoirs*
They were once intended to be a simple reserve of water for times of need,
but today the reservoirs are like a string of pearls in the mountain landscape. Especially idyllic: the *Embalse Cueva de las Niñas* in the *Pajonales*
nature reserve – a wonderful area for hiking and camping → p. 56

● *Fresh fish*
No matter how small the restaurant, they all serve fresh seafood. Of
course, fish always tastes best not far from where it was caught where
there is a fresh sea breeze and the tang of salt in the air such as on the
terrace of the *Casa del Mar* in Puerto de las Nieves → p. 64

● *Living monument*
The essence of the Canaries: if you take a stroll through the narrow
streets of *Teror*, cross over the *plaza* with the ancient laurel tree and
relax over a cup of coffee in one of the bars, you will get the feeling of
days long past → p. 71

● *Not only for botanists!*
The 2000 different plants that grow in a gorge below Tafira Alta can
be found nowhere else on earth! Among the many wonderful species
cultivated in the *Jardín Canario*, you will see dragon trees, various types
of spurge and dazzling red campanulas that are threatened by ex-
tinction → p. 43

# BEST OF ...

### ● Cold shivers included
Even museum haters will like this one: the *Museo Canario* in Las Palmas is the perfect place to be introduced to the world of the island's original inhabitants. The well-preserved mummies make an especially strong impression → p. 37

### ● Everything under one roof
You will not be bothered by the bad weather outside when shopping in Las Palmas' two main shopping malls *Las Arenas* and *El Muelle*. There are countless trendy shops next to each other and the latest blockbusters are shown in the cinemas (photo) → p. 29

### ● The battle of the big boys
Join Canarios of all age groups and cheer on the heavyweight stars – both men and women – at the *terreros de la lucha canaria* where competitors use rather unorthodox holds to throw their opponents to the ground → p. 22

### ● Experiments please!
You can get into the right mood for your visit to the *Museo Elder* in Las Palmas on the museum's fabulous homepage and find out what awaits you there: an interactive journey to the secrets of everyday life → p. 37

### ● Grand opera
Las Palmas has two wonderful concert halls and world-class musicians fly in to perform here – in the *Teatro Pérez Galdós,* beneath a ceiling of eroticised frescoes and in the *Auditorio Alfredo Kraus*, a fortress on the beach → p. 39 and p. 41

### ● Go under water
The best place to be if it rains is underwater! The 'Yellow Submarine' leaves Puerto de Mogán and goes down to the sea bed where you will be able to watch trumpet fish through large portholes swimming around a sunken ship – and stay completely dry → p. 89

RAIN

●●●●○ Dots in guidebook refer to 'Best of ...' tips

# RELAX AND CHILL OUT
## Take it easy and spoil yourself

● *Enjoy weightlessness*
It patters, gurgles and murmurs: let yourself be massaged by water jets or float in warm salt water in the *Gran Spa Corallium* in Las Meloneras. Afterwards relax looking out at the Atlantic through the large panorama windows. The spa in the neighbouring *Villa del Conde* Hotel has similar facilities → **p. 79**

● *Country hotel off the beaten track*
A romantic oasis lies hidden behind a natural stone wall several feet thick in Vega de San Mateo. Leaf through a book under a lemon tree, relax on the sunbeds at the pool or enjoy the open fire – in *Las Calas,* you will feel far away from the normal holiday hustle and bustle → **p. 73**

● *Sunset lounge*
A haven on white Amadores Beach: when the sun sinks into the sea behind Tenerife, you can relax at the *Amadores Beach Club* with an expertly mixed *mojito* in your hand. Reclining on soft cushions, your gaze will roam across the ocean at twilight → **p. 93**

● *Mens sana in corpore sano*
The *Talasoterapia Canarias* health centre in San Agustin pampers your body and soul from a to z – from Ayurveda to Zen. And if you feel like a massage, the hydro jets in the enormous pool filled with 36 degree saltwater will do the trick → **p. 94**

● *Cruising the coast*
Feel the sea breeze up your nostrils and relax with a view of Gran Canaria's coast from the water. A number of boats chug back and forth between Arguineguín, Puerto Rico and Puerto de Mogán all day long → **p. 93**

● *Mix with the locals*
Enjoy your *café con leche* on the terrace of *Quiosco San Telmo* in Las Palmas with a view of palm trees and dragon trees on the square. The pavilion itself is a real eye-catcher: pure Art Deco (photo) → **p. 38**

INTRODUCTION

# DISCOVER GRAN CANARIA!

It's the same picture every morning: men armed with machetes at work in the banana plantations, tomato harvesters picking their aromatic crop, fishermen setting out to sea in their boats, or shepherds in their traditional woollen cloaks taking their flocks up to higher pastures. Whether in La Aldea de San Nicolás in the west or Agüimes in the east, life follows a relaxed pace in most towns and villages on the island. Houses are clustered around churches and the shady plazas in front of them serve as playgrounds for children and meeting places for the elderly.

The capital, Las Palmas, with its networks of streets, seems light years away. The holiday resorts in the south, where a virtually invisible but perfectly functioning machinery ensures that the almost 2.5 million guests from all over Europe feel at home, seems similarly far removed. An armada of people – from the taxi driver who takes guests to the airport in the early hours of the morning and the cleaning woman who makes sure that the hotel rooms are 'like new', to the lifeguard who keeps an eye on the beach from his watchtower – take care of all of the holidaymakers' wishes. The

Photo: The dunes of Maspalomas

staff is not purely Canarian but international. Many come from the Spanish mainland and North Africa, from other European countries and South America.

Of course there are ugly hotel buildings that were thrown up in a hurry without much imagination and some of the shopping centres have becoming rundown over time. But efforts have been made over the past few years to brush up the island's image. Quite a few hotels have been revamped and have now become quite hip, spacious resorts with every comfort; others have been erected in the new resorts of Las Meloneras and Playa Amadores and are modelled on castles or African citadels. Visitors will find everything that is in fashion today; from golf courses, Asian-inspired therapy centres and yoga workshops to Pilates and Nordic walking on the beach. Holidaymakers staying in a finca in the middle of the island can go for hikes along restored trails and get to know the people and the countryside. Gran Canaria tries to please all tastes. It caters to those who are looking for the all-inclusive packages found in the resorts, as well as people who want to spend their holiday in the mountains, in one of the villages on the coast, or in Las Palmas, far away from tourist centres.

## For a long time, Gran Canaria was only Las Palmas

There are hardly any traces left of how Las Palmas once looked when the Spanish conquistador Juan Rejón landed on the island on 24 June, 1478 with his 600 followers, to claim the third largest Canary island – after Tenerife and Fuerteventura – for the Castilian crown. Wide beaches lined the northeast of the island, which covers 15322km (5922mi) and a fast-flowing river raced down to the coast. For five years the Canarians of old struggled to fight off the conquerors, but the Europeans, with

**1st century AD**
Pliny the Elder (23–79AD) describes the expedition to a group of islands he calls 'Canaria' in his 'Historia Naturalis'

**1478**
The Spanish conquistador Juan Rejón lands on the island on 24 June, 1478 and founds the settlement of Las Palmas

**1479**
The Alcáçovas Treaty cedes the Canaries to the Castilian Crown

**1483**
After several long battles, Rejón conquers the two realms on the island ruled by the Guanartemas clan

Dazzling white houses as a backdrop to the Sunday market in Teror

their modern weapons, were ultimately successful. Over the next few centuries, however, most changes on the island were restricted to Las Palmas and its immediate surroundings. The island experienced the boom – and then the decline – of the sugarcane industry. Shipping between Europe and South America made the city wealthy but also meant that pirates attacked the prosperous harbour. Gran Canaria was Las Palmas. The rest of the island was bitterly impoverished.

The island only really started to flourish with the introduction of tourism. Its rapid development into one of the largest holiday resorts in Europe started in the south in the early 1960s. Hotel complexes and resorts for more than 100,000 guests

**Magnificent flowers in an arid mountain landscape**

sprang up between San Agustín and Puerto de Mogán and there is no end in sight to this expansion. The beaches and dunes are simply too inviting, the good weather too stable, and the location between the mountains and sea too ideal. However, many

**1492**
Columbus stops at Gran Canaria on his first expedition to America

**1537**
The slave trade, that had decimated the native Canarian population following its conquest, is banned

**1820**
Las Palmas is officially named the capital of Gran Canaria

**1884**
Opening of the first hotel in Las Palmas

**1927**
Gran Canaria, Lanzarote and Fuerteventura unite to form the province of Las Palmas de Gran Canaria

tourists are shocked at how barren the south of the island is when they arrive at the airport in Gando. Only endemic flora brave this arid climate: *cardón* (column euphorbia), retama, tabaiba and tajinaste – thick-leaved, bushy cacti that can store water for long periods – have adapted to the conditions in this dry region. However, as soon as holidaymakers reach their accommodation they will be delighted by the profusion of flowers, made possible by lavish irrigation projects, and many tourists never leave the more luxuriant parts of the island during their entire stay.

## From deforestation to environmental protection

That is a real pity because there are many other facets to Gran Canaria. The island is of volcanic origin, almost circular in shape and the 1949m (6394ft)-high Pico de las Nieves, the highest point in the *cumbre* – the central mountainous region – rises up almost exactly in the middle. From here, valleys formed by erosion branch out to the coast. *Calderas* – bowl-shaped craters – bring back memories of days when there was still volcanic activity. No other Canary island is as rugged and furrowed with *barrancos* – the name given to the deep gulches on the archipelago – as Gran Canaria. In the south, they are parched by the sun and, with their bare, ochre-coloured rocks, appear austere and almost hostile. They only take on colour in spring when broom bathes them in a dazzling yellow. By contrast, in the north, these gullies often look like subtropical Gardens of Eden with lush plants that attempt to outshine each other with their beautiful blooms. This is where oranges, lemons and bananas grow, and cress, pumpkins and cabbages flourish on terraced fields.

Long ago, the island was covered by Canarian pine trees. Laurel tree forests drew moisture out of the clouds of the passing trade-winds that was absorbed by the ground and made the island fertile. The vegetation was absolutely unique. This sensitive ecosystem was initially damaged by the Spaniards who needed wood to build ships and then by the monoculture of modern farming. The Canarios started establishing nature reserves in the 1990s. There were also plans for a large national park in the centre of the island but the farmers and shepherds in the mountains were afraid that their already meagre earnings would be further diminished. Fortunately, a compromise was reached and the area has been protected as a Unesco Biosphere Reserve since 2005.

**Since 1950**
Tourists arriving by air rapidly lead to a boom period

**1982**
The Canaries are granted restricted autonomy and a regional constitution

**1986**
Spain becomes a member of the EU

**2010**
The Canaries are severely affected by the economic crisis; the unemployment rate rises to almost 30 percent

Impressive basalt monolith: Roque Bentaiga was sacred to the native Canarios

Those who take the time will be able to enjoy all that Gran Canaria has to offer. The island delights its visitors with magical beaches, breathtaking dunes and a wild mountainous region with the Pico de las Nieves as its highest point. The best views are to be had near Los Pechos. The lower mountain slopes in the north are covered with forests. It almost looks as if you could reach out and touch Spain's highest mountain, Teide, on the neighbouring island of Tenerife. There are not many native animals: lizards rustle through the underbrush, pigeons and a few birds of prey have the sky to themselves. The original canaries – small yellowish-green birds – wing their way through the woods. There is more variety under water. If you go snorkelling, you might even come across a manta ray and there are sharks, dolphins and grey whales in the 4000m (13,000ft)-deep trenches between the islands.

Initially, the Canarios had a hard time with Europe – and even with Spain. There was a separatist movement until well into the 1970s. But, that is all history now. Funding from Brussels has considerably improved

**The sun shines all year long**

the infrastructure of the towns and villages. Las Palmas has the flair of a modern metropolis but you can still experience the peace and quiet of rural life in the villages and small towns. Artenara is a well-preserved cave village, but the real eye-catcher is Teror. The ensemble of the old basilica, cobblestoned streets and the façades of the houses with their magnificent wooden balconies has been completely preserved and is considered the most perfect example of Canarian architecture. Explore the museums and churches on the third-largest island in the Canaries, take part in a pilgrimage or the magnificent carnival, and savour the traditional cooking and heady wine. Dive, go hiking, wind surfing, have fun all night long or just relax. You will never be bored on Gran Canaria. And all of this with sunshine – all year long.

# WHAT'S HOT

**1** Out and about

*Royal paths* The *caminos reales* used to be the only transport routes on the island. These are now enjoying a renaissance – as trekking and hiking trails. Almost 300km (200mi) have been restored already. *Freemotion* in Playa del Inglés *(Avda. Alféreces Provisionales s/n, photo)* offers guided hikes. Rustic country hotels, such as *Casa Rural Los Escobones* in the Parque Rural de Doramas *(Montaña Alta)*, are ideal starting points for a hike through the wilderness.

## African adventure

**2**

*African roots* With its candidature to become the 'European Capital of Culture 2016', Las Palmas rediscovered its African character and is now promoting its 'black' roots. The Africa House is investigating some lesser-known facets of its neighbours with cultural events held in the 19th-century palace *(Casa África, Calle Alfonso XIII 5, www.casafrica.es)*. Works by artists from Africa are also being exhibited in the *Centro Atlántico de Arte Moderna (Calle Los Balcones 9–11, www.caam.net)*.

## Paddling around

**3**

*Fast and furious* Paddle tennis, a mixture of the classic game and squash, is all the rage in *Gloria Palace San Agustín (Calle Las Margeritas s/n, Playa San Agustín, www.gloriapalaceth.com, photo)*. The *Tennis Center Maspalomas* has also reserved some space for this trendy sport *(Avda. Tour Operador Tjaerborg, s/n, San Bartolomé de Tirajana, Maspalomas)*. Sports shops have all the right equipment and a fine selection of paddles can be found in the *Al Campo Shopping Centre (Autovia Gran Canaria, Telde, Las Palmas, www.alcampo.es)*.

# Digital art

**Pictures and photographs** The art scene has discovered high tech. *Daniel Pérez*, who reworks his photos on the computer until the original forms disappear and a completely new picture emerges, is at the vanguard of this movement *(www.fdanny. eu)*. This new kind of art is on display in the *Galería Espacio Digital (Calle Cádiz 34, Las Palmas,* photo) and the *Galería Luroa (Calle Perdomo 10, Las Palmas)*. The *International Art and Digital Cultures Festival of Gran Canaria* provides up-and-coming artists with a platform *(www.canarias mediafest.org)*. The online culture magazine *www.frozzenmagazine.com* is well worth reading. It highlights international graffiti and video artists, graphic artists and architects, and takes its readers into studios where there is not an easel in sight.

# Party time

**Las Palmas' Old Town** The island's capital has had a facelift. Following the redevelopment of the historical city centre, chic bars and trendy restaurants have opened their doors in the vibrant shopping and entertainment district *Triana (www.zonatriana.com)*. There is always something happening here: *Cava de Triana (Calle Travieso 35)*, with its excellent wine and air-dried salami, and *La Butaca (Plaza Alameda de Colón 1)* are popular meeting places for the local 'in' crowd. Students drink their afternoon coffee in *Las Ranas Bar (CC Boulevard Monopol,* photo) and things really get moving there later at night. *Bar Cuasquías*, in an old, lovingly-restored stone building *(Calle San Pedro 2)* is also a real hotspot.

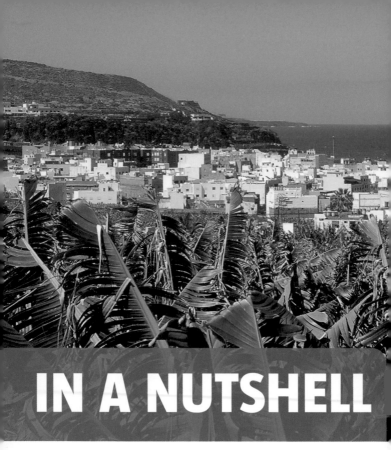

# IN A NUTSHELL

## BANANAS

Gran Canaria has an ideal climate for bananas and there have been large plantations on the island for a good 100 years. The landscape near Arucas and around Arguineguín is covered with banana plants. After the harvest, workers cut down the trunks and young plants sprout out of the ground. Canarian bananas are smaller than Central American ones but have much more flavour. The weekly market in Las Palmas is a good place to find them.

## BUILDING FREEZE

The economic crisis succeeded in achieving what laws had not been able to accomplish – a building freeze. On Gran Canaria this has led to many beautiful stretches along the coast being left untouched – for the time being. Spanish banks used to be very generous in granting loans but they have now become extremely restrictive. And, without loans, there is very little building activity because modest wages and the high level of unemployment mean that few households have any additional income from savings. The banks have long started to feel the consequences of their former liberal lending policies: many Canarios are no longer able to meet their obligations and their flats and houses have been repossessed by the

Photo: Banana plantation in Arucas

Set out on a voyage of discovery: from the dunes to the snow, from *carnaval* to *lucha Canaria*

banks that are now struggling to get rid of them at considerably reduced prices.

# CAMELS

It looks like something out of the Arabian Nights when you see a long caravan of camels making its way through the dunes near Maspalomas. The animals have become a major tourist attraction. The one-humped dromedaries probably arrived on Gran Canaria with the first Europeans. The ideal work animals – they can go for weeks without water and carry heavy loads without complaining – were used for many things. Although it seemed that their careers had come to an end with the introduction of machinery, camels experienced a renaissance through tourism. are three camel stations on the island; dromedaries are bred near

Fataga which you can visit to see young animals at close quarters.

# CARNAVAL
★ *El carnaval* is something very special on Gran Canaria. It is a fiesta full of fantasy, for all the senses, during which, once a year, the Canarios throw all the confining norms of everyday life completely overboard. Preparations for the festive season start months before the actual event that always takes place in February and March. *Carrozas* (festive floats) are built and decorated, costumes stitched, masks and disguises modelled. Every village has its *murgas*, costumed groups of clowns who parade through the streets singing and dancing during the *desfiles*, the processions. The fun usually only begins in the evening and continues all through the night. Agüimes is the centre of rustic carnival life. The processions in Las Palmas are more elaborate and the coronation of the *reina del carnaval* (Carnival Queen) is shown live on television: the costumes of the contestants often cost as much as a middle-of-the-range car. Each carnival day ends with a *mogollón*, dancing to Latin rhythms until the early hours of the morning. The *entierro de la sardina* – burial of the sardine – is the magnificent end to all the celebrations. Nobody really knows why a fish is carried to its grave. But it is a good reason for one final procession through the streets with a gigantic cardboard sardine; the rousing finale comes about when it explodes in a dazzling display of rockets and firecrackers.

# CAVES
Many people in Artenara, high up in the mountains, still live in cave dwellings – just as they did 1000 years ago. And, if they have to, they simply chisel a new room into the soft tuff rock. Nowadays, however, they don't tackle this with picks and axes as they did in great-grandfather's days although, in principle, not much has changed. Of course, they now have water and electricity but it is still not possible to dig too deep into the rock because moisture could enter. The people living in these cave dwellings appreciate their advantages. They are warm in winter and cool in summer. Another positive aspect is that if you build your house in the rock, it will have little impact on the landscape. The old-Canarios built their homes in caves in the rocks, buried their dead there, and used them for storage and rituals as can be seen most impressively in Cenobio de Valerón. There are also many caves that were once lived in and used as burial sites in the Barranco de Guayadeque near Agüimes.

# DONKEY'S STOMACH
*'Panza del burro!'* (donkey's stomach) is what the Canarios call the clouds blown in by the trade winds that gather and build dense banks in the north of the island. The origin of this name is rather curious. Many of the locals' ancestors were farmers and, in the olden days, almost all of them had a donkey that was used as a draught and pack animal. When it became hot at midday and siesta time approached, farmers used to lie down beneath their donkeys to get some shade. Looking up, they only saw the animal's white and grey stomach. This did not have the same colour as the trade wind clouds, but hung just as low!

# DRAGON TREES
There is a magnificent specimen of the most mysterious Canarian plant on a small plaza not far from the basilica in Teror. The dragon tree, *drago*, is the island's emblem. Its 'dragon blood' – the tree's resin turns dark red when it comes into contact with the air – was used for preparing medicines. Gran Canaria even has an

# IN A NUTSHELL

endemic species that can only be found here and nowhere else in the world – not even on the other Canary Islands. The plant, which only grows in the difficult-to-reach gorges in the southwest, was named after the pre-Hispanic island name *Dracaena tamaranae* (Gran Canaria was known as 'Tamarán' until 1483). The 'normal' dragon tree however is much more widespread and appears in many village names: El Dragonal, El Draguillo and Dragos. There is a magnificent grove of dragon trees in the *Jardín Canario* botanical gardens near Las Palmas.

## DUNES

The shimmering, golden white *Dunas de Maspalomas* are an absolutely unique natural phenomenon. The walls of sand rise up to a height of almost 12m (40ft). The more than 1000 acres of sand and its endemic flora have been protected as a natural landscape of national interest since 1987. Although many people believe it, they were not created by sand from the Sahara 200km (125mi)

away across the ocean but almost entirely from coral and shells that were ground by the waves and washed ashore. And, they move – albeit at a snail's pace – 2–5m a year towards the west, and a continuously reshaped and patterned by the trade winds. This movement is only stopped by the increase in vegetation and weaker winds further away from the sea.

## LUCHA CANARIA

Canarian wrestling, *lucha Canaria*, was already popular in the days of the first Canarios. It is only practised on the seven islands of the archipelago. Twelve fighters from two teams wrestle in pairs against each other in a ring approximately 15m (50ft) in diameter covered with sawdust or sand. The *luchadores* use various unorthodox holds to get the better of their opponent and throw him to the ground in a maximum three-minute bout. Not only weight, technique and speed play a major role. *La lucha Canaria* now takes second place to football on the island and is still very popular with extensive televi-

Today, many people still make their homes in caves in Artenara

Lucha Canaria: the first to hit the dust, loses

sion coverage given to major tournaments. There are ● *terreros de la lucha canaria,* wrestling arenas, in Puerto de Mogán, Ingenio, Gáldar, Firgas and Las Palmas. Tourist information offices have details of forthcoming fights.

# SNOW
It might seem an absurd topic when talking about an island off the coast of Africa, but snow falls every two or three years in Gran Canaria's *cumbre,* the rugged mountainous regions around the 1949m (6394ft)-high Pico de las Nieves. And, it is a real sensation whenever it happens. It makes the headlines of the daily newspapers and local television companies send teams of reporters into the mountains. And, at the weekend, thousands of Canarios set out to have snowball fights, build snowmen and queue for a cup of hot chocolate at one of the mobile stands to warm themselves up.

# THE FIRST CANARIANS
Not much is known about the original inhabitants of the Canary Islands. They probably first settled on the islands sometime after the 5th century BC and were descendants of light-skinned Berbers from North Africa or – as more recent genetic research considers possible – from the Mediterranean area near Sicily. The islands soon lost contact with each other. Boat building was unknown, and fishing was only carried out from the shore. The original Canarians were mainly farmers who tended sheep and goats and cultivated barley that they used to make *gofio* flour for their staple food. Two kingdoms established themselves on Gran Canaria: one in the northwest with Gáldar as its capital and one in the northeast in the area around Telde. They were ruled over by the Guanartemas clan. Most of the people lived in caves, where they also frequently buried their dead who had been mummified with great skill. When the Spanish landed in 1478, Tenesor Semidan ruled in Gáldar and Doramas in Telde. After five years of battle, the conquistadors succeeded in conquering the local population. Tensor Semidan was taken captive and allowed himself to being baptised. The

decimated population became absorbed by the Spanish.

## VIRGEN DEL PINO

The *Romería Virgen del Pino*, the 'Pilgrimage to the Virgin of the Pine', the largest on the island, is held in Teror on two days at the beginning of September. The pilgrimage has its origin in a legend that the Virgin Mary appeared to Canarian shepherds nearby on 8 September, 1481 and that, shortly afterwards, they discovered a figure of the Mother of God in a pine tree. A chapel was built, pilgrims started to arrive and Teror developed into the place of pilgrimage it is today. In addition to the solemn procession during which the highly revered, splendidly attired statue of Mary is carried through the streets of Teror, the fiesta held on the day before is a fascinating event every year. Groups of people in traditional costume and in magnificently decorated carriages come from all of the villages on Gran Canaria, as well as from the other islands, to pay homage to the Virgin Mary. The day ends with a cheerful fiesta with merry-go-rounds and stands selling all kinds of specialities that lasts all night long.

## WATER

There is a drawback to an island where the sun always shines: the lack of water. There used to be rivers on Gran Canaria with dense laurel forests drawing moisture out of the trade winds and wells supplying water for the farmers. Now, the trees have been cut down, the wells have dried up and there is only one small stream on the island. Rainwater is collected in gigantic reservoirs that often appear to be threateningly empty. That made the invention of desalination plants so important for Gran Canaria. It became possible to make use of an inexhaustible resource – the ocean – instead of digging ever deeper into the ground to tap the meagre groundwater supply through mile-long galleries. Only a few years ago, the salt had to be removed using expensive, oil-driven equipment but now this takes place using the environmentally-friendly process of osmosis. However, this still costs a lot of money and requires a great deal of energy. So please try to not waste water!

## WINE

Wine growing has a long tradition on the Canary Islands. It seems that the first vines were brought to Gran Canaria from Crete in the 15th century. Shortly afterwards, European dynasties did all they could to get their hands on the wine made from the heady Malvasier grapes. The biggest client was England and you can still read about how enthusiastic people were about the high-quality tipple in Shakespeare's plays. However, Spanish-English competition put an end to the good business. Phylloxera was another problem that caused Canarian wine production to decrease dramatically and it soon only had symbolic importance. This all changed when Spain entered the EU and enormous subsidies were made available. The Canarios have rediscovered their old wine, small family wineries have been modernised and new bodegas opened. Today, wine is no longer only grown in the traditional El Monte region between Santa Brígida and Bandama but all over the island: in the mountainous region near Fataga and San Bartolomé de Tirajana in the south, as well as in the northwest in the Agaete valley, in the east near Telde and even high up near the mountain peaks. The grapes are harvested in September so that the young wine can be tasted along with freshly roasted chestnuts on St Martin's Day at the beginning of November.

# FOOD & DRINK

**The chef recommends: *potaje canario*, a hearty vegetable soup, and *gofio escaldado*, fish stock bound with cornflour**

Bread and a bottle of Firgas mineral water to go along with it – *buen provecho!* And a healthy appetite is also a plus. It is only a pity that these tastily prepared dishes seldom find their way onto the menus of tourist restaurants; they are the best way to get a feeling for real Canarian life.

The islanders themselves always cook simple dishes but with that extra something. This is no wonder seeing that the first Canarians had to try to make something out of the little they had. The water-mills in the mountains rattled away day and night to grind roasted grain into flour that was stored in large sacks piled up against the walls. A nondescript, beige-coloured powder trickled out of them: *gofio*, the staple food of an entire people. Whether made of barley, wheat or corn, *gofio* flour was always available; it could be stored for a long time, used for a great variety of purposes and was rich in protein. It was baked into bread and tortillas, stirred into soups and sauces, and eaten along with fish and meat.

Today, stews and soups, combined with leftovers from other meals, still form the basis of the *cocina casera* – the Canarian

Photo: The restaurant Montesdeoca in Las Palmas

## Dine like the Canarios: *gofio*, fish and spicy sauces form the basis of Canarian cooking – a fusion of dishes from three continents

home-style cooking – that is so popular in simple restaurants. Especially at lunchtime, between 1pm and 3pm, workers tuck into a cheap meal. Visual refinement and sophisticated service are secondary. All that's important is that it is quick, the white bread is fresh and that the servings are generous. Fish is usually served *a la plancha*, simply grilled on both sides in a little olive oil. This is how they like their

*vieja* (parrot fish), *caballa* (mackerel), *sama* (brace) and *cherne* (perch) – and you can be sure that Canarian fish is always freshly caught.

The *cocina casera* also reflects the time when the Canaries were at the crossroads of two worlds. Yams from Africa, sweet potatoes from South America and saffron from La Mancha are all found in modern dishes. Caribbean *arroz a la cubana* –

# LOCAL SPECIALITIES

▶ **adobo** – spicy marinade with oil, laurel leaves, herbs, white wine, peppers, garlic and pepper in which meat is left to soak for several days

▶ **baifito en adobo** – kid marinated in *adobo* and then roasted, served with *papas arrugadas* and salad, is a traditional Christmas meal

▶ **bienmesabe** – thick, golden-brown dessert made of honey, almond slices, egg yolk and lemon

▶ **caldo de pescado** – light fish soup with potatoes and herbs

▶ **carajacas** – finely sliced calf's, pig's or chicken's liver, usually marinated in *adobo*

▶ **gambas al ajillo** – shrimps in olive oil, spiced with garlic, pepperoni and parsley

▶ **gofio escaldado** – fish broth thickened with cornflour

▶ **leche asada** – pudding made with boiled milk and eggs, lemon peel and cinnamon

▶ **mojo rojo** – 'red mojo' a spicy creamy or liquid sauce made of red pepperoni, oil, garlic, vinegar and salt

▶ **mojo verde** – 'green mojo' is similar to *mojo rojo* but with green instead of red pepperoni and a lot of parsley

▶ **papas arrugadas** – small, extremely starchy, Canarian potatoes cooked in very salty water; they are always eaten with their wrinkled (Spanish: *arrugado*) skin (photo left)

▶ **potaje de berros** – mild, cress stew with bacon, potatoes, maize, pumpkin and yams. *Gofio* is served with this and you add as much as you want

▶ **potaje de cardos** – soup made with the leaves of wild thistles harvested in the mountains in spring; slightly bitter

▶ **rancho canario** – hearty stew with chickpeas, potatoes, pork, noodles, onions, saffron, garlic and paprika sausage

▶ **ropa vieja** – thick stew made of leftovers and chickpeas, meat, vegetables and potatoes – a traditional farmer's dish

▶ **sancocho canario** – fish preserved in salt and then boiled, served with vegetables and *mojo*

a creation of rice, tomato sauce, fried banana and fried egg – is very popular in traditional eateries. However, only the finest restaurants still take the trouble to make traditional dishes such as cress and thistle soup and *carajacas*; dishes that are often determined by the season and are complicated to prepare correctly. The Canaries have also fallen victim to the law of raking in the money, meaning that many restaurants in the tourist areas prefer to earn their living with bad *paella* rather than with seasonal, regional cooking.

In contrast to lunch, breakfast is rather spartan. It often just consists of a *café solo* (espresso) or *cortado* (with a little milk) and that often not at home but knocked back standing at the bar in a cafeteria. The latest gossip gets spread while guests eat a *bocadillo* – a bread roll with ham or cheese – prepared by the barman, and then it's a quick *ta luego* and off to work. When tourists go to local restaurants in the evening, they often find themselves alone. While many people from the north of Europe tuck in sometime between 6pm and 8pm, the Spaniards prefer to have a *merienda* – a snack of a few tapas, for example – to tide them over until later. The Canarios usually do not sit down to eat dinner with their families until about 9pm or 10pm when the temperature is more pleasant.

You can still find traditional Canarian dishes in good restaurants. *Cherne al cilantro* (perch with coriander) or *en esabeche* (in a spicy sauce), *conejo en salmorejo* (rabbit in laurel marinade) and *baifito en adobe* (kid in garlic) are traditional Canarian specialities you should try. The chef of the *Las Grutas de Artiles* restaurant in Santa Brígida, which serves the best traditional cooking on Gran Canaria, still sets out for the island's eastern wine region at the start of the harvesting period to make sure that he gets a few barrels of the outstanding *Del Monte* wine. The royal families of Europe used to be fond of wines from Gran Canaria and

some connoisseurs' eyes still grow misty thinking about them, although wine from the Spanish peninsula now dominates the market on the island. There are countless varieties of Canarian cheeses and they all go well with a glass of wine. The

Pavement café in Las Palmas

cheese is made from unpasteurised goat's, sheep's or cow's milk – or a mixture of all three – characterised by three levels of ripeness: *tierno* (fresh, mild), *semicurado* (semi-mature) and *curado* (mature). *Queso de flor* is absolutely unique; the addition of thistle juice makes this the most unusual cheese on the Canaries.

# SHOPPING

Don't worry if you suddenly remember that you have no souvenirs just before you are due to take off! You can buy a taste of the Canaries in the departure hall of the airport after you have checked in: from almond-honey mousse and olive oil from Temisas and Arucas Rum, to chorizo sausages from Teror. There are even strelitzias in special boxes that will fit into the overhead lockers on the plane.

## ARTS & CRAFTS

Guía in the north of the island is well known for its fine wood carvings. Intricate articles are woven from the fronds of the Canarian date palm. Particularly in Ingenio, charmingly simple bags, hats, mats and bread baskets are made this way. Pottery also has a long tradition on the Canaries. Rustic ware for everyday use is made without a potter's wheel: sieves, jugs, vases, pots for onions and garlic, carafes and bowls. The elaborate lace tablecloths and scarves, as well as embroidered articles, are also of very high quality. *FEDAC*, a state-run shop with the aim of promoting local arts and crafts is a address to note for those interested in Canarian arts and crafts *(www.fedac.org)*. They sell *cuchillos canarios*, Canarian knives with artistic intarsia handles, handbags woven out of palm fronds, archaic hand-shaped ceramics, silver and lava jewellery, lace and embroidered tablecloths in all sizes, and many other articles. The quality is exceptional, the designs often unique. There are FEDAC branches in Las Palmas (Triada), Cruz de Tejeda and Playa del Inglés.

## INDOOR & OUTDOOR MARKETS

Market stands are set up once a week in many villages where you can buy groceries and fruit and vegetables as well as ceramics, embroideries and woven goods. There are three market halls in Las Palmas. The largest is *El Mercado Central* in the Catalina district near the port with two floors of the freshest products imaginable: stacks of avocados, papayas and mangos, artichokes and yams, small and large potatoes, herbs and spices. Meat and fish are also sold on the ground floor where the goods are a little more expensive.

Arts and crafts and culinary delights – there is room for lava jewellery or honey rum in any suitcase

## SHOPPING CENTRES

The best place to shop is in the capital, Las Palmas. On your way stop off at one of the largest and most-beautifully located outlet stores in Spain: the *Centro Comercial Las Terrazas* lies directly on the sea! It has shops run by famous fashion labels as well as a large electronics market *(www.centrocomerciallasterrazas.es)*. There are two attractive shopping centres in the beach and port districts of Las Palmas itself. ● *El Muelle* and ● *Las Arenas* have all international top brands as well as cinema complexes, bistros, cafés and fast-food restaurants. There are also shopping centres in the holiday resorts in the south but you will hardly find any quality brands there. The *Centro Comercial Boulevard* on the promenade in Las Meloneras is an exception with its high-price boutiques and jewellery shops.

## SWEETS

*Turrón* from Teror, a nougat-like delicacy, is sold in all colours at roadside stands in and near the town. *Ron con miel*, honey rum from Arucas (*Indias* is the best brand) is a potent souvenir. Excellent *bienmesabe*, the delicious Canarian dessert made of honey and almonds, can be bought in supermarkets (*Tejeda* brand).

## WINE

You can buy wine from Gran Canaria in any well-stocked supermarket but the largest selection is available in the *El Corte Inglés* department store in Las Palmas. Make sure to buy wine labelled *Denominación de Origen* (protected mark of origin) – only then can you be certain that the wine has been produced in a hygienic environment exclusively with local grapes.

# THE PERFECT ROUTE

## GRAIN CAVES AND CHEESE SNACKS

It is best to speed past the not very attractive eastern coast on the main road from the south, GC-1, and then bypass ❶ *Las Palmas* → p. 32. Follow signs to Gáldar/Agaete. A detour to the ❷ *Cenobio de Valerón* → p. 68 (photo left) will bring you onto the dramatic old mountain road, GC-291. From afar, you will be able to make out a split mountain with caves just the height of a man, where the indigenous Canarians used to store their surplus grain. Continue on to ❸ *Santa María de Guía* → p. 68 which is famous for its 'flower cheese'. You can try it in many places including Señor Carmelo Súarez' bar El 7 and then enjoy a stroll through the historical streets of the town.

## RUINS AND SARDINES

One of the loveliest church squares is in ❹ *Gáldar* → p. 62. The ruins of the ancient Canarian capital city in the archaeological park are even more fascinating. You can take a break at the sandy beach in the small village of ❺ *Sardina del Norte* → p. 64 for a quick swim and then enjoy a seafood lunch.

## BETWEEN THE MOUNTAINS AND THE SEA

Oranges and lemons grow along the side of the road that leads down from ❻ *Agaete* → p. 65 into the valley. The road becomes narrow and very twisty beyond the Los Berrazales Hotel and the landscape increasingly untamed. Driving back through the ❼ *Valle de Agaete* → p. 65 you will have frequent glimpses of the sea that you eventually reach in ❽ *Puerto de las Nieves* → p. 64. Take a stroll from the old harbour wall past the terrace restaurants on the promenade; they all serve delicious fish dishes.

## FANTASTIC CLIFF ROAD

The GC-200 opens up Gran Canaria's wildest stretch of coast. The mountains reach down to the sea and plummet abruptly into the depths. You have a wonderful view across the water to Tenerife from the ❾ *Mirador de Balcón* → p. 51! If you have become a bit dizzy after the 300 bends, you can recover in ❿ *Puerto de la Aldea de San Nicolás* → p. 52 and relax with a refreshing walk along the seaside promenade.

## FROM DIZZYING HEIGHTS DOWN TO THE BEACH

The climb up into the mountains starts after you pass the ⓫ *Cactualdea* → p. 50 cactus park. From the top of the pass at a height of 700m (2230ft), you have a good view back to Agaete valley where you will see the enormous sheets of plastic covering

the fruit and vegetable plantations; there is a complete contrast in the other direction – impressive steep rock faces and gorges as far as the eye can see. Drive past the mountain village of Mogán until you reach the coast. The old houses in the fishing village of ⑫ *Puerto de Mogán* → p. 88 cling to the slope like swallows' nests. A walk through the streets full of flowers with a view of the port and the sleek yachts at anchor makes a refreshing break! The road along the cliffs takes you back to ⑬ *Playa Amadores* → p. 92 (photo below left) where you should stop for a dip in the sea. After you have dried off, drive back past Puerto Rico and Arguineguín to the south coast: the quickest route is via the GC-1, but the old coastal road, GC-500, is much more beautiful even if it does take a while longer.

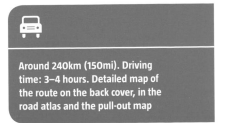

Around 240km (150mi). Driving time: 3–4 hours. Detailed map of the route on the back cover, in the road atlas and the pull-out map

# LAS PALMAS

**MAP INSIDE BACK COVER**
(131 D–E 1–3) (*[]] H 2*) **A city in the fast lane. While all other major centres in Spain are cutting back, Las Palmas has increased its culture budget. One festival follows another and new museums are being opened.**

Even if Las Palmas is not chosen to become the 'European Capital of Culture 2016', all the activities undertaken to back its candidature will have done the city a lot of good. No matter whether it is the production of Wagner's 'Ring des Nibelungen', whacky street theatre à la Fura dels Baus, contemporary art or modern design: the cultural scene is amazingly dynamic.

Las Palmas is more than 500 years old. When the Spanish conquistador Juan Rejón and his 600 soldiers dropped anchor off

> **CITY WHERE TO START?**
> **Plaza Santa Ana:** It is best to take the bus to *Vegueta*, the Old Town. The express buses 30 and 50 connect the south of the island with Las Palmas. Park your car near the market *(mercado de la Vegueta)* or in the multi-storey car parks in the shopping centres near the beach *(Las Arenas/ El Muelle)*. Taxis are expensive!

---

Photo: The port of Las Palmas

## More than 500 years of history: Gran Canaria's capital city between colonial times and the new millennium

the coast of the Isleta, the small peninsula on the north coast of Gran Canaria, on 24 June, 1478, he found only volcanic rock and enormous sand dunes. The army then moved southwards to the Barranco de Guiniguada where a powerful river flowed coastwards. Rejón established a settlement there under the high palm trees that were to give the city its name – *Ciudad Real de Las Palmas*, Spain's first colonial city. Rejón originally called it Vegueta, the 'small meadow'. And today, more than 500 years later, you can still feel the charm of time gone by in Vegueta, especially at weekends when there is less traffic. Every step you then take resounds on the cobblestones around the cathedral on tranquil *Plaza del Pilar Nuevo* and the wide *Calle de los Balcones*, where Castilian gentlemen once rode past elegant colonial buildings. The pace of life in Vegueta is slow. *Plaza de Santa Ana* is only full when mass is held in the cathedral – at other times it seems well and truly given over to the city's pigeons.

The hustle and bustle has also remained. For the Canarios, Triana is a synonym for shopping and browsing for hours on end in the continuously expanding pedestrian precincts that, along with the small streets

The Triana pedestrian precinct is the perfect place for a relaxed shopping spree

What a difference when you cross the wide dual carriageway – where a river once flowed, by the way – and enter *Triana*! The commercial district of Las Palmas was also founded by the Spaniards but it represents a completely contrasting world. This is where foreigners settled – the Dutch, Portuguese and English – who came to Gran Canaria during the sugar boom. Fortunes were made and invested; change and growth took place at a dizzying pace. With the arrival of the English at the end of the 19th century, most of the colonial buildings in Triana were replaced in the fashionable Art Nouveau style. Some can still be admired today – for example, the splendid façades on *Calle Mayor de Triana*.

and squares where traffic is limited, represent the most delightful aspect of life in Las Palmas.

The 'Port of Light' *Puerto de la Luz*, almost 6km (4mi) to the north, was not always part of Las Palmas. This is where merchant ships stopped over on their way from Europe to America. The port brought prosperity to the city but people did not want to live there. The upper-class created its own green 'garden city', *Ciudad Jardín*. It is still Las Palmas' most exclusive district; a luxuriant oasis of flowers and white villas. The end of the 20th century witnessed a reckless construction boom. High-rise apartment buildings can be seen from afar; satellite suburbs were erected on the slopes of the hills to provide homes for the many people seeking their luck here. Las Palmas has a population of 380,000 and is by far the largest city in the Canaries. However, it has long been recognised that things cannot go on like this and major renovations have been undertaken where rapid success seemed most likely such as on *Las Canteras* beach, where there are countless cafés and restaurants on its almost endless promenade. And, tranquil areas have been created near the *Parque Santa Catalina* by banning traffic. This also applies to the Old Town where ugly roundabouts and bridges were removed and road tunnels have taken their place to give pedestrians more room.

It is a good idea to leave your car in one of the multi-storey car parks and explore the city on foot, by bus or taxi. Las Palmas is full of traffic wardens just waiting to hand out tickets or have your car towed away.

## SIGHTSEEING

For only 15 euros, you can ride on the open tourist bus *guagua turística* from one sight to the next for a full day and get on and off wherever you wish. Descriptions of the various attractions are also given in English. The red double-decker buses depart from Parque Santa Catalina between the port and Las Canteras beach *(daily 9.30am–5.45pm, every second hour | eleven stops)*.

### CAAM ●

The *Centro Atlantico de Arte Moderno* displays modern art (sculptures, paintings, objects) in a sober setting on its five floors of exhibition space. It is hidden behind the façades of the old houses on the best-preserved street in Vegueta, the *Calle de los Balcones,* behind Santa Ana Cathedral. Temporary exhibitions and lectures. *Tue–Sat 10am–9pm, Sun 10am–2pm | admis-sion free | Calle Los Balcones 9–11 | www.caam.net*

### CASA ÁFRICA ●

The Africa House was opened in an impressive colonial building from the 19th century in 2008. It presents works by artists from the neighbouring continent: paintings, films and music, and is located halfway between the Old Town and Ciudad Jardín. *Mon–Fri 9am–2pm and 5pm–8pm, Sat 10am–2am | free admission | Calle Alfonso XIII 5 | www.casafrica.es*

### CASA CONSISTORIAL

The Old Town Hall opposite Santa Ana Cathedral was reopened with great pomp – today, it is only used for representational purposes. The showpiece is the Golden Hall

## MARCO POLO HIGHLIGHTS

★ **Casa de Colón**
Magnificent colonial building with two romantic patios
→ p. 36

★ **Museo Canario**
Where you can find out everything about the first inhabitants of the island → p. 37

★ **Montesdeoca**
Fairy-tale atmosphere and exquisite food In Las Palmas' most captivating restaurant → p. 39

★ **Playa de las Canteras**
Fun and games on the almost 3km (1¾mi)-long beach and promenade → p. 41

★ **Santa Catalina**
Where the king stays. Colonial charm in one of the oldest hotels on Gran Canaria → p. 43

(*Salón Dorado*) with its frescos and stucco work. The most impressive of the many artworks is the painting 'The Emigrants'. It shows Canarios embarking ships for America where they hoped to find a better life. *Currently only open on Sat morning | admission free | Plaza Santa Ana*

## CASA MUSEO PÉREZ GALDÓS

Furniture that used to belong to the Canarian writer Benito Pérez Galdós, who was born here in 1843, as well as his works, are displayed in one of the last remaining 18th-century houses in the Triana district. *Mon–Fri 10am–2pm and 4pm–8pm, Sat–*

The magnificent wooden balconies of the Casa de Colón in the Old Town of Las Palmas

## CASA DE COLÓN ★ ●

The 'Columbus House' is a magnificent colonial building; the oldest sections date from the 17th century. This is where the Spanish Governor used to reside. The covered wooden balconies and oriels of Canarian pine are typical of the islands. The *celosía* shutters are especially note-worthy and provided air-conditioning of a kind in the olden days. The delicate wooden latticework lets air in but blocks out the sun and heat. The museum shows exhibits from the Spanish *conquista* as well as numerous artefacts from pre-Columbian days and Columbus' journeys. *Mon–Fri 9am–7pm, Sat–Sun 9am–3pm | admission free | Calle Colón 1*

*Sun 10am–2pm | admission free | Calle Cano 6 | www.casamuseoperezgaldos.com*

## CASTILLO DE LA LUZ

This small fortress was built by the Spaniards in 1493 to protect the Isleta. It played an important role in defending Las Palmas from an attack by the English fleet under Sir Francis Drake in 1595. It is now planned to establish a museum for modern art in the building, focussing especially on the work of Martín Chirino. Chirino was born on Gran Canaria in 1925 and is con-sidered to be the most widely known 20th-century Spanish sculptor. *Opening times were not known at the time of print-ing | Calle Juan Rejón s/n*

## CATEDRAL DE SANTA ANA

Construction of the main church in Las Palmas with its five naves began in 1497 but had to be interrupted in 1570 for lack of money. Building was not completed until the early 19th century. This is reflected in the architecture of the house of worship. The ribbed vault is Gothic, the façade Neoclassicist. There is a Baroque altar and works by various Canarian artists inside. Please remember that taking photographs and talking is taboo during church services. *Visits only in connection with the Museo Diocesano de Arte Sacro. Visits to the tower: Mon–Fri 10am–4.30pm, Sat 10am–1.30pm; mass: Mon–Fri 8am–10am, Sat–Sun 8am–9.30am and 6pm–8pm | entrance fee 1.50 euros; free during mass*

## ERMITA DE SAN ANTONIO ABAD

The hermitage, the oldest church in Las Palmas, took the place of the chapel in which Christopher Columbus prayed in 1492 before he set out on his voyage to the New World. *Plaza de San Antonio Abad*

## GABINETE LITERARIO

The first theatre in Las Palmas opened its doors in 1844 and was redecorated in the purest Art Nouveau style at the end of the 19th century. Today, readings and exhibitions are held in its sumptuous halls. *Plaza de Caraisco*

## MUSEO CANARIO ★ ●

The museum of Canarian history has the most extensive collections of finds from Antiquity on the Canary Islands. These include the 'Idol of Tara', a clay female figure that probably symbolises fertility. There is also a replica of the *Cueva Pintada* from Gáldar, as well as scenes of everyday life. In addition: skulls, skeletons and several well-preserved mummies. *Mon–Fri 10am–5pm, Sat–Sun 10am–2pm | entrance fee 3 euros | Calle Doctor Verneau 2 | www.elmuseocanario.com*

## MUSEO DIOCESANO DE ARTE SACRO

The church museum with religious objects, as well as a small gallery of paintings, is attached to Santa Ana Cathedral. *Mon–Fri 10am–4.30pm, Sat 10am–1.30pm | entrance fee 3 euros | Calle Espíritu Santo 20*

## MUSEO ELDER ●

The museum of science and technology is located in a hall that was formerly used for storing shipping goods. The three floors show exhibits – some of them interactive – dealing with space travel, mathematics and physics, Canarian flora and old, as well as alternative forms of technology. *Tue–Sun 10am–8pm | entrance fee 5 euros | Parque de Santa Catalina | www.museoelder.org*

## MUSEO NÉSTOR

This small museum, opened in 1956, is an oasis of tranquillity and art in the midst of the busy Pueblo Canario. It displays works by the Canarian painter Néstor Martín Fernando de la Torre (1887–1938) as well

Museo Canario: the Idol of Tara

as designs for houses, furniture and stage settings. *Tue–Sat 10am–8pm, Sun 10.30am–2.30pm | entrance fee 2 euros | Pueblo Canario, Parque Doramas | www.museonestor.com*

## PARQUE DE SANTA CATALINA

Las Palmas' largest square is a large area – most of it paved – where many of the city's main events including its carnival are held. During the day, most of the activity takes place in the shade of the palm trees in front of the houses around the square. You can watch the Canarios going about their everyday life from the pavement cafés. A sculpture made of tiles at the southern end of the square shows the flags of the all of the world's countries.

## PARQUE DORAMAS

A sculpture in this small park commemorates the early-Canarian King Doramas who fought against the Spaniards before being ultimately defeated. There are also allusions to the legendary collective suicide of the final survivors, who leapt to their deaths from Fortaleza de Ansite near Santa Lucía.

## PARQUE SAN TELMO

All buses arrive and depart from the underground terminal here. Above the ground, you will find a pavilion where you can get a map of the city and a description of its most important sights. There is a playground for children and quiet corners where you can take a rest. The highlight is a second Art Nouveau pavilion, the graceful ● **INSIDER TIP** *Quiosco (open at varying times)* that houses a small café with wood-panelled walls.

## PLAZA DE SANTA ANA

This is the main square in Vegueta. The administrative buildings of the church and crown were located around the square after the time of the Spanish *conquista*; the *Catedral de Santa Ana* and the *Casa Consistorial* lie facing each other. The eight bronze, almost 100-year-old, dogs in front of the cathedral seem to be guarding it.

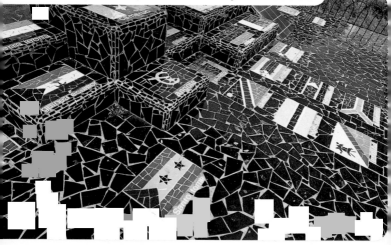

A colourful sculpture in the Parque de Santa Catalina with flags from around the world

## PUEBLO CANARIO

The intention to show visitors to Las Palmas a real Canarian village became too idealised. Construction of the cramped complex with a church, craftsmen's workshops, a cafeteria and other buildings started in 1939; however, some of the delicately carved oriels and shutters as well as decorative portals are of interest. *Folklore performances at 11.30am on Sun | in Parque Doramas*

## TEATRO PÉREZ GALDÓS ●

This splendid theatre opposite the *mercado* was erected in 1919 in a mixture of colonial and Art Nouveau styles. It used to be the cultural centre of Las Palmas. A modernistic cubic extension, which harmonises well with the old *teatro*, was added during the many years of restoration and now concerts and opera and theatre performances are held here once again. There is a monumental sculpture of Benito Pérez Galdós (1843–1920), Gran Canaria's most famous writer, on the remodelled plaza in front of the theatre. Many of his realistic novels – including Viridiana, Tristana and Nazarín, all filmed by Luis Buñuel – have found their place in the canon of world literature. *Calle Lentini | www.teatroperezgaldos.es*

## FOOD & DRINK

### EL HERREÑO

This restaurant near the *mercado* in Vegueta is renowned for its wide selection of tapas, simple dishes and low prices. It is very popular with the locals and is always busy. *Open daily | Calle Mendizábal 5 | tel. 9 28 31 05 13 | Budget–Moderate*

### EL PADRINO

Something very different: Canarios in particular are fond of this restaurant on the Isleta. Things are pretty lively in the winter garden with its jungle of greenery. Fish is the highlight. *Open daily | Las Coloradas | tel. 9 28 46 20 94 | Moderate*

### INSIDER TIP ▶ LA MARINERA ≈

Its prime location at the northern end of Las Canteras beach attracts lots of people. No matter whether you sit inside or out, you will be right on the water. The emphasis is on fish, the cooking is exquisite and the view of the pounding waves will take your breath away. *Open daily | La Puntilla | tel. 9 28 46 88 02 | Expensive*

### INSIDER TIP ▶ LE VOLANT ≈

This is the place to dine on creative Canarian cuisine in a minimalistic environment high above the city in Hotel AC Gran Canaria. Inexpensive buffet lunch *(Mon–Fri)*. *Open daily | Calle Eduardo Benot 3 | tel. 9 28 27 37 45 | Expensive*

### MONTESDEOCA ★

This elegant restaurant is located in an old palace. Well preened waiters serve classical international cuisine in a romantic inner courtyard full of greenery. Chamber music is occasionally performed at the weekend – the perfect address for an elegant night out! *Closed Sun | Calle Montesdeoca 10 | tel. 9 28 33 34 66 | Expensive*

## SHOPPING

### EL CORTE INGLÉS

The traditional department store is a paradise for well-heeled shoppers. The building on the northern side is especially interesting; this is where you will find fashion articles and cosmetics as well as the longest fish counter in the Canaries in the grocery department in the basement. The artistically arranged sea creatures are continuously moistened with a fine spray of water. The wine shop has all of the is-

As fresh as it gets: the cornucopia of fresh produce in the *mercado*

land's best vintages; the cheese section sells the Canaries' finest cheeses –including the famous 'flower cheese' *queso de flor*, of course! And you can try before you buy: just say 'Podría probar un trocito?'. The selection in the adjoining delicatessen department is even more exquisite. This is where you can buy the very best (and most expensive) goods Spain has to offer. *Mon–Sat 10am–10pm | Avenida Mesa y López | www.elcorteingles.es*

### INSIDER TIP ▶ FEDAC

A very special address: the finest Canarian arts and crafts from woven handbags and ceramics to silver jewellery, lace and embroidered tablecloths, in a side street off Triana. Exquisite, traditional, new – and even recycled – goods. *Mon–Fri 9.30am–1.30pm and 4.30–8pm | Calle Domingo J. Navarro 7 | www.fedac.org*

### INSIDER TIP ▶ LA LIBRÉRIA

This small bookshop is devoted exclusively to the subject of Gran Canaria. There are good hiking guides, maps and background literature in many languages. *Mon–Fri 9.30am–1.30pm and 4.30–8pm, Sat 9.30am–1.30pm | Calle Cano/corner of Matula*

### MERCADO CENTRAL

Shopkeepers sell the island's freshest produce on the two floors of the Central Market – in the Catalina district near the beach. This is the place to buy fruit and vegetables, herbs and spices; things are a little more expensive on the ground floor where you will also find fish and meat. *Mon–Sat 8am–2pm | Calle Galicia 14*

### MERCADO DE LA VERGUETA

The market in the old part of the town is where Vergueta's heart beats. The stands are tightly packed next to each other in the huge hall; shoppers and visitors jostle their way past them. There are not only fruit and vegetables, but also a large selection of meat, fish, cheese and sausages. *Mon–Sat 8am–2pm | Calle Mendizábal*

## MERCADO DEL PUERTO

The pace is somewhat slower in this architecturally interesting iron construction à la Eiffel near the port than in the markets in the old part of town. You can also buy flowers and second-hand articles here. *Mon–Sat 8am–2pm | corner Calle Tenerife/ Calle Albareda*

**INSIDER TIP** RASTRO

The Sunday flea market near Parque Santa Catalina attracts thousands of visitors every weekend. There is an enormous range of articles: wooden African masks, whole-grain products from the local Zipf bakery, Spanish fashion made in China, kitsch and commerce, as well as a few snack bars and live music – that makes rummaging around real fun!

## BEACH

One hundred years ago, bathers could already be seen strolling across the fine white sand of the ⭐ *Playa de las Canteras* in the wide bay of Las Palmas. Today, it is characterised by the same urban flair shared with the other large city beaches worldwide. 3200m (2mi) of powdery sand line the several small bays that combine to create a broad arch beneath the wide promenade. A reef protects the beach from surging waves, but they are still high enough at the southern end to make surfing possible.

The fortress-like concert house the ● *Auditorio Alfredo Kraus* dominates the scene with the pyramid roofs of the *Las Arenas* shopping centre behind it. Las Canteras is often compared with the beaches of Rio de Janeiro and it actually has a lot of the Brazilian city's vivacity. This is guaranteed by all of the cafés, restaurants, shops and snack bars that line the promenade. There are also public showers and WCs.

## ENTERTAINMENT

If you are not staying in Las Palmas, you should only come here on Friday or Saturday nights for fun; at other times, there is not much going on.

You will find large cinemas that show the latest films in *Las Arenas (southern end of the Canteras promenade)* and *El Muelle (Muelle Santa Catalina)* shopping centres. The locals chill out between Plaza de Caraisco and Triana in the *Boulevard Monopol*, a small shopping centre with pubs, sandwich shops and cocktail bars. The most popular is *La Taberna* with a spacious terrace and subdued pop music. A new pub district has become established opposite this in *Vegueta (Calle Mendizábal)* with bars (including *ECAbiss*), *tascas* and pubs that are especially popular with students.

After midnight, the action moves to *Santa Catalina* and the beach area. The 'Bermuda triangle' with discos (such as *Palacio Lutino*), pubs, snack bars and amusement arcades is between *Parque Santa Catalina, Calle Luís Morote* and *Calle Nicolás Estévanez* and *Las Canteras*. In summer, the *Playa*

## LOW BUDGET

▶ You can visit the ● *Catedral de Santa Ana* without paying while mass is being held (Mon–Fri 8–10am, Sat/ Sun 8am–9.30am and 6pm–8pm). This makes the experience particularly impressive.

▶ Admission to the state museums in Las Palmas – and most of them are – is free of charge; this includes the *Casa de Colón*, the *CAAM* and the *Casa África*.

de las Canteras is jam-packed until late. The beach cafés are open well into night as are the *cervecerías*, pubs that not only serve beer.

rolled into one. There is always something happening: on Fri and Sat, there is usually live alternative music – from jazz and funk to rock; once a week, the inter-

Twilight on Plaza de Caraisco; chilling out before night falls

### INSIDER TIP CC EL MUELLE

At night, the shopping centre opposite Santa Catalina Park flashes and sparkles like a pinball machine. This is where Las Palmas' young crowd comes to have fun until the small hours. There are rows of countless pubs, such as *Terraza Kopal* and *Limerick*, on several open levels with a view of the port. At the very top, under the tented roof, the open-air discos don't really get going until after midnight.

### LA ESTACIÓN

The glazed 'station', with *Pepa*, the train that connected Las Palmas with the port one hundred years ago, is the location with the most variety in town. It is a café, snack bar, pub and stage for live bands

national Erasmus students hold parties here. *Daily 10am–3am | Plaza Santa Catalina near Museo Elder*

### INSIDER TIP PARANINFO

The Paraninfo has been an important meeting place for many years and each generation has its own new impulses. Music from hard rock and reggae to Latino is played on several dance floors and there are live concerts on some nights during the week. The atmosphere is completely laid-back: there is no dress code and no bouncer at the entrance. There is also usually not much action before 1am, but then the party lasts until the crack of dawn. *Tue, Thu–Sat 11pm–5am | Calle Franchy y Roca 17 | www.salaparaninfo.com*

**INSIDER TIP ▶ PEQUEÑA HABANA**

Young couples sway to classical Latin rhythms in this lively salsa disco on Plazoleta de Farray. *Wed–Sun 10pm–4am | Calle de Fernando Guarnateme 45*

## WHERE TO STAY

**FATAGA**

Average standard hotel opposite the main market near the Mesa y López shopping area and only about 500m from the beach. The Evolución rooms have a uniquely contemporary feeling to them: you enter through the open bathroom that is only separated from the sleeping area by glass. Good breakfast buffet with sweet fare from the hotel's own shop. *95 rooms | Calle Néstor de la Torre 21 | tel. 9 28 29 06 14 | www.hotelfataga.com | Moderate*

**LUZ PLAYA**

The 34 modern, functional, bright flats are located directly on the beach promenade. *Calle Sagasta 66 | tel. 9 28 26 75 50 | www.luzplaya.com | Budget*

**NH IMPERIAL PLAYA**

The location directly on the beach is the main selling point of this comfortable ho tel. *142 rooms | Calle Ferreras 1 | tel. 9 28 46 88 54 | www.nh-hoteles.es | Moderate*

**REINA ISABEL**

Las Palmas' best beach hotel on Playa de las Canteras; comfortable, modern and with a large swimming pool on the rooftop terrace. *400 rooms | Calle Alfredo L. Jones 40 | tel. 9 28 26 01 00 | www.bullhotels.com | Expensive*

**SANTA CATALINA** ⭐

The top hotel in Las Palmas is also one of the oldest on the island. It was built in 1890 in the colonial style with old wooden balconies, an elegant club bar and a mag-

nificent terrace café. The Spanish king is a frequent guest. The rooms are a little dark but the princely breakfast buffet and a spa with an indoor/outdoor pool as well as Finnish and steam saunas more than make up for it. *Calle León y Castillo 227 | tel. 9 28 24 30 40 | www.hotelsantacatalina.com | Expensive*

## INFORMATION

**PATRONATO DE TURISMO**

The main tourist office is located on one of the central thoroughfares near the Parque de San Telmo and there are several information kiosks throughout the city. *Calle León y Castillo 17 | tel. 9 28 21 96 00 | www.grancanaria.com*

## WHERE TO GO

**JARDÍN CANARIO** ●

(131 D3–4) (*M G 3*)

The 'Canarian Garden' covers the side of a hill in the Barranco de Guiniguida below Tafira Alta. Its official name is *Jardín Botanico Canario Viera y Clavijo* after a Canarian historian. The park is an oasis of peace where mainly endemic plants such as the dragon tree, *palmera canaria* and Retama are cultivated. The succulent garden, where some of the cactus-like specimens are as big as trees, is impressive. There are small ponds with birds. It is a very popular destination for families at weekends; the ⚜ **INSIDER TIP** *Jardín Canario* restaurant *(open daily | Plan de Loreto | tel. 9 28 43 09 39 | Moderate)*, with excellent Canarian cuisine and a unique view into the valley, is located at the upper entrance. Daily 10am–6pm | *free admission | entrance: at km 7 on the GC 100 between Las Palmas and Tafira Alta; alternative, more convenient, entrance on the GC 310 between Tamaraceite and Tafira Alta. Both are signposted. 7km (4½mi)*

# CENTRAL REGION

A cool breeze wafts through the airy pine forests; groves of fig and medlar trees provide shade; apricots and other fruit flourish in small plantations and a dusting of snow covers the mountains – it may be hard to believe but this is Gran Canaria.

Many people forget that the *cumbre* (mountain peaks), as the mountainous area of the island is called, reaches a height of almost 2000m (6500ft). On average, the temperature on *Pico de las Nieves*, at 1949m (6394ft) the highest spot on Gran Canaria, is usually 10–20 degrees lower than on the coast. Although the changing climate means it seldom

happens, old people still talk about winters when they could not open the doors of their isolated homes high up in the mountains as so much snow had fallen during the night. While holidaymakers make sure they have enough t-shirts and shorts with them, those living in the mountains always have a woollen hat and thick jacket close at hand between December and February.

Life in this rough environment is not easy. The barren, rugged *cumbre* seems a dangerous place. And when the dark clouds move across and give the rocks and ridges a threatening air, it is easy to understand how the poet Miguel de Unamuno thought

Photo: View of the church in Santa Lucía

## Wild gorges and precipitous peaks: man takes second place to nature in Gran Canaria's rugged mountainous regions

of this as a *tempesta petrificada*, a 'petrified storm'.

Life in the central region of the island, far from the flood of tourists that characterises the south, is still very traditional. Many people on the northern side of the *cumbre*, which the trade winds provide with more moisture than the south, still make a living by cultivating vegetables, fruit and grain. For centuries, generations skilfully carved terraced fields into the steep slopes where the delicious small potatoes grow particularly well.

Village life takes place between the field, the local bar and the family. The locals are more reserved than those on the coast. Of course, the land has made the people the way they are and the most fascinating aspect of this region is its tranquility.

# ARTENARA

**(129 E4)** *(⏍ D 3)* ★ ☆ **Some 1500 people live in Artenara – most of them still in cave dwellings. The most recent were created only 30 years ago but the oldest are several centuries old.**

The native Canarians knew what they were doing. When the Italian architect Leonardo Torriani visited the homes of the island people in 1590, he noted that "... old people, the nobility and kings live in caves

Gran Canaria can get pretty cold in winter. The best place to study the architecture is from the road to Tejeda where there are some goat stables in the caves. Twisty footpaths lead up the rock face from where you can admire the view into the wide *Barranco de Tejeda* with *Roque Bentaiga* and *Roque Nublo* behind it. Artenara's centre is near the church on the hilltop where there is more room and the streets and squares are generously laid out. Fortunately for Artenara, there are hardly any ugly new buildings.

The cave chapel 'Virgen de la Cuevita' was carved out of the rock

in order to enjoy the warmth stored in the pores of the earth in winter and to be able to escape from the hot rays of the sun and refresh themselves in summer." The microclimate in a cave is absolutely unique. This is especially advantageous in Artenara. Located at a height of 1270m (4170ft) above sea level, the highest village on

## SIGHTSEEING

### IGLESIA SAN MATÍAS

This colonial church is in the middle of the pedestrian precinct. The large barrel vault in the central nave, with its fine wooden coffered ceiling of Canarian pine, is unusual for Gran Canaria. *Open daily*

**INSIDER TIP** VIRGEN DE LA CUEVITA ●

This cave chapel – an 860ft² room carved into a vertical fissure – is devoted to the guardian saint of folk musicians and cyclists. Bench-like niches were chiselled into the rock; a raised oriel was reserved for the village dignitaries. The confessional, altar and pulpit were also worked out of the tuff. *Accessible on foot or by car from the plaza along the steep uphill lane. The chapel is always open. Please close the wrought iron gate after your visit!*

## FOOD & DRINK

### LA ESQUINA 〰️〰️

Lovely location in the centre of the village. Panoramic view into the valley from the terrace where hearty Canarian food is served. The restaurant is occasionally overrun by groups of tourists. *Closed Sun | near Mirador | tel. 9 28 66 63 81 | Moderate*

**INSIDER TIP** MESÓN MIRADOR LA CILLA 〰️〰️

The most charming restaurant in Artenara was closed for many years before it re-opened in 2011. It is reached through a 50m long tunnel above the church; a terrace with a magnificent view of the mountains opens up at its end. The food – Canarian cuisine with a lot of meat – is only of minor importance. *Open daily | Camino de la Cilla 8 | tel. 9 28 66 62 27 | Moderate*

## WHERE TO STAY

Artenara is one of the main centres of *turismo rural*, tourism in the countryside off the beaten package holiday track. There are several holiday flats in and near the village – most of them in fully equipped houses and fincas.

### CUEVA DE LAS MARGERITAS

The completely renovated cave dwelling lies on a steep slope near fields and vineyards. *2 rooms | Calle Las Aruejas 38 | tel. 6 49 99 26 36*

### EL CAIDERO 🕐

Large, bright cave house on the edge of the village. The eggs for breakfast are provided by the chickens running around outside. *Calle El Caidero 8 | www.artenatur. com | Moderate*

## INFORMATION

### INFORMACIÓN TURÍSTICA

Of course, the tourist information office is also located in a cave – that alone makes it worth a visit! *Calle Párocco Domingo Báez 13 | tel. 9 28 66 61 02 | www. artenara.es*

⭐ **Artenara**
Cave village at a dizzying height
→ p. 46

⭐ **Pinar de Tamadaba**
The trade winds delicately caress the largest pine forest on the island → p. 48

⭐ **Pico de las Nieves**
Magnificent panoramic view from Gran Canaria's highest peak → p. 49

⭐ **Tejeda**
The delightful mountain village and the massive Roque Bentaiga lie opposite each other → p. 54

⭐ **Roque Nublo**
Fantastic views on a hike to Cloud Rock → p. 57

**MARCO POLO HIGHLIGHTS**

# CRUZ DE TEJEDA

## WHERE TO GO

### CALDERA PINOS DE GÁLDAR
(129 E4) (*𝄢 E 3*)
Take the GC110 from Artenara towards Vallesco; the wide crater (Spanish: *caldera*) of the extinct volcano comes into view about half way along the route (7km/4mi) through the green regions of the north. The smooth, sparsely vegetated, slopes are covered with *picón*, small lava stones, and ash and plummet steeply to the bottom of the crater. You will be able to make out fissures and erosion in the solid magma stone. The forest becomes denser as you continue with your journey. The rocks are now covered with moss and ferns nurtured by the deciduous trees that lose their leaves in winter. The best-cultivated terraced fields on Gran Canaria can be seen in the *Barranco de las Lagunetas* where the road leads up to Cruz de Tejeda. *12km (7.5mi)*

### PINAR DE TAMADABA ★ ☆
(129 D 3–4) (*𝄢 C–D 3*)
The largest forested area on Gran Canaria is made up almost exclusively of *pinus canariensis*, the Canarian pine. The tall tree has adapted itself perfectly to surviving in the volcanic environment over millions of years. The thick bark that once protected the trunk like a fireproof jacket from the heat of the falling ash, does the same today against forest fires. In this way, even trees that are completely singed on the outside are still alive and come into leaf again after a blaze. The thin, green, very long needles draw water from the passing trade winds that then fall to the ground. The long lichens hanging like an old man's beard from the branches on the north slopes where the trade winds are strongest are especially noteworthy. They are nourished entirely by the clouds.
If the weather is fine, it is a good idea to interrupt your tour of the west of the island and walk as far as the steep slope. From there, you have a fantastic view of the neighbouring island of Tenerife and Spain's highest mountain – the 3817m (12,523ft)-high Teide. Naturally, it is also possible to make this tour on foot or by bike; there are several picnic areas on the way. *10km (6mi)*

# CRUZ DE TEJEDA

(129 F5) (*𝄢 E 4*) **Tejeda Cross is not a village but the most important junction in the *cumbre* at a height of 1490m (4888ft).**
From here, roads fan out to all parts of the island. This is a very popular day-trip destination with holidaymakers and why you will find a surprising number of restaurants in such a small area.

## FOOD & DRINK WHERE TO STAY

### EL REFUGIO
This Alpine-style mountain lodge is a real gem for holidaymakers seeking something out of the ordinary. The guesthouse has ten rooms – all of them decorated differently – a small garden and a mini swimming pool. Here, guests are still treated as friends. The hotel also has a good restaurant *(open daily | Moderate)* where guests are served hearty country cooking. Very popular with day trippers. Try *baifo* – spicy kid! *Tel. 9 28 66 65 13 | www.hotelruralelrefugio.com | Moderate*

### PARADOR CRUZ DE TEJEDA ☆
The mountain hotel in a manor house with a view of the *cumbre* was opened in 2009. Rustic atmosphere, large terrace, pool and

For a small tip you can take a ride on a donkey at Cruz de Tejeda

spa. The restaurant *(open daily | Expensive)* transforms local specialities into sophisticated, gourmet delights. There is also a fast-food cafeteria for those who want to eat relatively cheaply. The most magnificent view is from the INSIDER TIP *Parador's* terrace – your gaze wanders over pine-covered slopes to the abysses of the Caldera de Tejeda and as far as Roque Nublo and Roque Bentaiga on the opposite slopes. *43 rooms | tel. 9 28 01 25 00 | www.parador. es | Expensive*

## WHERE TO GO

### PICO DE LAS NIEVES ★ ●
🌤 (129 F6) (*Ø E 4*)

At a height of 1949m above sea level, the 'Snow Peak' is Gran Canaria's highest mountain – and, it occasionally snows here in winter. The panoramic views from the road across large sections of the island are really breathtaking. On clear days, it looks like you could reach out and touch Tenerife's Teide; from another stop, you can make out the small sister island Gomera

if you take your binoculars with you. On the opposite side of the mountain top, the *Pozo de las Nieves* (near the antennas), you might even be able to see the southern tip of Fuerteventura. It is not possible to climb to the peak itself; it is part of a military complex and a prohibited area. *8km (5mi)*

## LOW BUDGET

▶ You can have a ride on a donkey at *Cruz de Tejeda* – children especially will like this. It is free, but the owners of the animals have nothing against a small tip *(propina)*.

▶ A cup of coffee or a beer on the promenade at *Puerto de la Aldea* will cheer you up and not dent your holiday budget. The view of cliffs around the bay and the fishing boats coming back to port is free of charge.

# LA ALDEA DE SAN NICOLÁS

(128 B5) *(∅ B 4)* **This village stretches out over a fairly large plain, by Gran Canaria's standards, that is surrounded by high mountains on both sides.**

La Aldea de San Nicolás is the most isolated village on Gran Canaria and does not really belong to any part of the island. Until 2010, it could only be reached via a spectacular, but difficult to drive, road along the cliffs. But now EU funding is being used to build a road of tunnels and bridges that will shorten the distance from 'civilisation'.

From afar, you will get an idea of how most of the 8000 inhabitants make their living. Sheets of plastic, the size of football pitches, cover the land in a graphic pattern. These sheets create a microclimate that makes it possible to harvest tomatoes several times a year. La Aldea de San Nicolás itself is not the most attractive town imaginable; the small plaza near the church is the only really pleasant spot.

## FOOD & DRINK

### SEGUNDO
The bar is very popular with the locals. Tapas and good home-style cooking. The owner is also the proprietor of one of the only two hotels in San Nicolás. *Open daily | opposite the church* | Budget

## WHERE TO STAY

### HOTEL CASCAJO
Simple recently built hotel with 20 rooms; near the church. *Tel 9 28 89 11 65 (or enquire at Bar Segundo)* | Budget

### HOTEL LA ALDEA SUITES
Four-star hotel in the centre of town with 27 spacious country-style suites with balconies opening onto the pool and garden. *Calle Transversal Federico Rodríguez Gil s/n | tel. 9 28 89 10 35 | www.laaldeasuites. com* | Moderate

## WHERE TO GO

### CACTUALDEA (128 B6) *(∅ B 4)*
You can admire 100,000 cacti and other plants in the Cactus Village. In addition,

# A DIFFERENT KIND OF HOLIDAY

*Turismo rural*, rural tourism, is designed for people who want to discover the real Gran Canaria, far off the beaten track and unspoilt by mass tourism. Guests live like the locals in fincas, manors, country hotels and cave dwellings. This type of accommodation can be found in many villages and small towns, each house being fully equipped for those who want to cater for themselves. The minimum booking is for two nights. A good overview and additional information on *turismo rural* can be found on the very-well designed, multilingual website: *www.grancanaria. com/natural* operated by the *Patronato de Turismo (Calle León y Castillo 17 | Las Palmas | tel. 9 28 21 96 00)*. The *Asociación Canaria de Turismo rural (tel. 9 28 39 01 61 | www.ecoturismo canarias.com)* has a list of additional places to stay.

the – still relatively new – complex southeast of La Aldea de San Nicolás on the road to Mogán has cafeterías, a souvenir shop and a large pool of glittering stones that are sold by weight. A large selection of young cacti are also for sale. *(Daily 10am–5pm | entrance fee 6 euros | tel. 9 28 89 12 28). 4km (2.5mi)*

Cactualdea: be careful, very prickly!

### INSIDER TIP ▶ TRIP TO ARTENARA
(128–129 B–E 4–5) (*B–D 3–4*)

If you want to leave civilisation behind, take the GC 210 from La Aldea de San Nicolás to Artenara. What is almost certainly Gran Canaria's least travelled road is 30km (18½mi) long and often so narrow that two cars often can't pass. The road starts in the centre of San Nicolás (ask for *dirección Artenara*) and winds its way up to an altitude of 1300m (4265ft).

Initially, you drive through banana and avocado plantations with orange groves lining the roadside. After only a few hundred yards, the landscape changes completely. The road leads into the *Barranco de la Aldea*, a gorge that seems to have been taken from a Wild West film. The vegetation becomes stunted and sparse. If you stop, all you can hear are the birds in the rushes around flat ponds which are the only remains of the rivers that once washed enormous troughs out of the rock.

The road winds up through a series of hairpin bends, passing reservoirs that store rainwater. Just before you reach a tunnel, you will be taken aback by your first glance of the entire monumental panorama of the *cumbre*. The scene is dominated by Gran Canaria's two major landmarks, the monoliths *Roque Bentaiga* (on the left) and *Roque Nublo* (on the right). Broom and *tajinaste*, later medlars and almond trees, and finally well-tended terraced fields will make you aware of just how fertile the land is here. The façades

of the cave dwellings cling to the perpendicular rockface like swallows' nests.

The road enters the *Tamadaba* pine forest at an altitude of almost 1200m (4000ft). Artenara is not far away and it is certainly possible that you will not have met a single car coming from the other direction for the last hour or so. Mountain-

bikers can also tackle this tour. Real cracks start in La Aldea de San Nicolás but it is better to take the downhill route from Artenara if you are not so well trained. *30km (19mi)*

### MIRADOR DE BALCÓN ☼
(128 B4) (*B 3*)

The platform at this viewpoint on the coast road to the north was cut into the rock and provides those who stop here with an amazing view down to the raging

San Bartolomé de Tirajana: sleepy mountain village and political centre

sea below and along the steep coastline. *3km (1¾mi)*

### PUERTO DE LA ALDEA DE SAN NICOLÁS (128 A5) (𝄞 A–B 4)

The Port of La Aldea de San Nicolás consists of long stretch of rocky coast that is very popular with anglers, a promenade, a large harbour wall and a small dense forest of *pino marino* coastal pine. There are dozens of picnic tables in the shade of the trees and they are completely over-run by the locals at the weekend. Most of the few houses are also restaurants; they don't have much to keep them busy during the week but do serve good fish dishes. *Aguas Marinas* and *El Charco (open daily | Moderate)* are especially recommendable. *5km (3mi)*

# SAN BARTOLOMÉ DE TIRAJANA

**(134 B2) (𝄞 E 5) This unpretentious village existed back in the days of the original Canarios – when it was know as *Tunte*.**

The village of San Bartolomé, a small place with approximately 4000 inhabitants, is dominated by its charming little church, built in the 18th century and dedicated to Santiago, the patron saint of Spain. The artistically carved wooden ceilings in Mudéjar style in the three-nave house of worship are particularly noteworthy. This is also true of the several perfectly preserved portals made from the wood of the Canarian pine.

San Bartolomé is, however, a master of deception. There is no indication that this is also a seat of politics. This village in the mountains is actually the administrative centre of the entire south of the island from Bahía Feliz to Pasito Blanco and this means that enormous amounts of money pass through the council's hands. This also means that in the past some of the local dignitaries made a packet during the tourism boom and accusations of corruption can still be heard today.

## FOOD & DRINK

### LA PANERA DE TUNTE

The 'baker's wife' *(panera)* in Tunte – the old-Canarian name of San Bartolomé de Tirajana – not only sells delicious sandwiches, the ever-popular *bocadillos*, but also mouth-watering strawberry tarts. You can eat the inexpensive snacks on the spot in the café. *Calle Reyes Católicos s/n | Budget*

### INSIDER TIP PANCHO GUERRA

Hearty Canarian specialities, which have become rather rare on the island, are served in the restaurant and pretty patio that belong to the Hacienda del Molino next door. These included kid, *sancocho* (boiled salted fish) and rabbit. *Open daily | Budget–Moderate*

## WHERE TO STAY

### INSIDER TIP LA HACIENDA DEL MOLINO

This down-to-the-earth country hotel was once a mill. The eight rooms are all decorated differently; some have balconies, others are split-level but they are all rustically furnished. Excellent cooking. *Calle Los Naranjos 2 | tel. 9 28 12 73 44 | www. lahaciendadelmolino.com | Budget*

### PARADISE LAS TIRAJANAS ❄

This elegant manor-house hotel occupies a splendid position above the Fataga valley; it is ideal for biking and hiking tours and for active holidaymakers. In addition, the hotel offers many other sporting activities and has it own spa. *60 rooms | Calle Oficial Mayor José Rubio s/n | tel. 9 28 12 30 00 | www.hotel-lastirajanas. com | Moderate*

## WHERE TO GO

### EMBALSE DE CHIRA

(133 E2) (*ɷ D–E 5*)

The reservoir was created in a magnificent setting in a depression below a dense pine forest. A twisty road that offers many wonderful views of the countryside leads down to it. Two simple bars guarantee that day trippers don't go hungry or thirsty. *12km (7.5mi)*

# SANTA LUCÍA

(134 C2) (*ɷ F 5*) **The village with 1500 inhabitants is the centre of an area of scattered settlements in the upper section of the *Barranco de Tirajana*.**

Most people who live here in the fertile *barranco* are engaged in agriculture. The houses and farms lie in the midst of small palm groves and avenues of high eucalyptus trees scattered across the wide semicircle formed by the slopes. There is an impressive church from the early 19th century in the centre of the village; its tower crowned with a minaret is reminiscent of a mosque. Along the road there are a number of bars and small shops selling oranges and lemons, pickled olives and locally made goat's cheese.

The old people in Santa Lucía still tell of how, just two generations ago, use was made of the amazing acoustics to call across from one side of the mountain to the other more than 500m away, sometimes simply to ask relatives living at the other end of the village to drop by and bring a loaf of bread with them from the bakery when they came. Today, the patchwork of low white houses still appears to belong to a completely different era.

## SIGHTSEEING

### MUSEO CASTILLO DE LA FORTALEZA

Canarian history and folklore are the focus of this small private museum. The owner, who was a passionate collector, not only brought together farming equipment, plants and stones but also the mortal remains of his early-Canarian ancestors. They are now on display in a – really rather kitschy – mediaeval-style fortress (Spanish: *castillo*). *Daily 9am–1pm and 4pm–7pm | entrance fee 2 euros | on the through road*

## FOOD & DRINK

### HAO

The restaurant behind the museum has a good reputation for its typical Canarian cooking; it is also a destination for tourist buses. Guests sit outside on a spacious shady patio. *Open daily | tel. 9 28 79 80 07 | Moderate*

## WHERE TO STAY

### EL OLIVAR

This village house from the 16th century is in the centre of Santa Lucía. It has four separate holiday flats, terraces with a view of the valley and a garden with cacti and a shared pool and barbecue area. *Tel. 9 28 33 02 62 | www.santalucisrural.com/elolivar | Moderate*

# TEJEDA

**(129 E5)** *(Ø E 4)* ★ ⊯ **This village at an altitude of 2400m (3445ft) and with a population of 2400 is probably the most picturesque on Gran Canaria and very popular with camera-wielding tourists.** It lies spread over several hills and plateaus on the sun-flooded southern slope of a vast gorge, surrounded by high mountains. Its whitewashed houses with their green shutters and wooden balconies are typically Canarian. The church is surrounded by a maze of small streets, flights of steps and squares. Strolling along the main street, visitors feel just as relaxed as if they were on a promenade. All of this is made even more spectacular by the majestic *Roque Bentaiga* on the other side of the valley. The Almond Blossom Festival with stands and fireworks is held here in February.

## SIGHTSEEING

### CENTRO DE PLANTAS MEDICINALES ☺

A large number of the plants grown in the garden in front of the greyish-brown building of natural stone in the Centre for Medicinal Herbs are dried to make *infusiones* (herbal teas) – try a cup while you are there! The chemist's shop from the 19th century with its beautiful porcelain jars, old scales and weights, which was 'transplanted' here in its entirety, is a real highlight. Posters illustrate traditional forms of healing. *Tue–Sat 11am–3.30pm, Sun 11am–4pm | entrance fee 2 euros | Calle Párocco Rodríguez Vega 10 | www.plantasmedicinalescanarias.com*

### MUSEO HISTORIA Y TRADICIONES

Small museum focusing on local traditions in a lovely village house. *Tue–Fri 11am–3.30pm, Sat–11.30am–4pm | entrance fee 2 euros | behind the church*

Tejeda, up in the hills, is one of the island's most picturesque villages

### INSIDER TIP MUSEO TRES CRUCES

This is how the Canarios lived in times gone by: Paco Suárez displays historical everyday articles in his traditional house in the village. *Tue–Sun 11am–5pm | entrance fee 2 euros | in the lower section of the village*

## FOOD & DRINK

### CUEVA DE LA TEA

This inn serves hearty meals at tables outside on the pavement. *Closed Mon | Calle Hernández Guerra 21 | tel. 9 28 66 63 06 | Moderate*

## SHOPPING

### INSIDER TIP DULCERÍA DEL NUBLO

The delivery vans of this renowned confectioner are known all over the island. *Mantecados, piñones* and *mazapán,* Tejeda's marzipan cakes, will tempt those with a sweet tooth to visit the shop on the main street. Perfect souvenirs for loved ones back home. *Daily 9am–6pm | Calle Hernández Guerra 15*

## SPORTS & ACTIVITIES

Tejeda is an excellent place to set out on fascinating hikes into the interior of the island, to *Pico de las Nieves* or to *Pajonales,* Gran Canaria's largest nature reserve, for example.

## WHERE TO STAY

### APARTAMENTOS GAYFA

The two spacious holiday flats have a living room, bedroom, kitchen and bathroom, as well as a spectacular view deep into the valley from your terrace. *Calle Hernández Guerra 17 | tel. 9 28 66 62 30 | Budget*

### HOTEL FONDA DE LA TEA ☺

This comfortable country hotel in a painstakingly restored manor house more than 100 years old, is in the centre of the village. The eleven rooms are bright and cheerful (satellite TV, heating) and breakfast is served in the rustic restaurant. There is a magnificent view of the jagged mountains from the communal terrace and a fire blazes in the hearth in the salon in the evening. The hotel management stresses environmental friendliness – everything that can be, is recycled. *Calle Ezequiel Sánchez 22 | tel. 9 28 66 64 22 | www.hotel fondadelatea.com | Moderate*

## INFORMATION

### INFORMACIÓN TURISTICA
A museum showing the work of the sculptor Abraham Cardenes who was born in Tejeda is attached to the tourist information office. *Mon–Fri 11am–3.30pm, Sat–Sun 11.30am–2.30pm | Calle Leocadio Cabrera 2 | tel. 9 28 66 61 89 | www.tejeda.es*

## WHERE TO GO

### AYACATA (129 F6) (𝔐 E 4)
This small village on the southern side of the *cumbre* is famous for the almond blossom that blooms in Jan and Feb. Down-to-earth home-style cooking can be found in the pleasant *Casa Melo Restaurant (open daily | tel. 9 28 17 22 61 | Budget)* – but ask the price before you order! *12km (7.5mi)*

### EMBALSE CUEVA DE LAS NIÑAS ● (133 D 1–2) (𝔐 D 5)
The idyllic reservoir is located to the south of Ayacata in the *Pajonales* nature reserve. It is also possible to pitch your tent here

# BOOKS & FILMS

Although Gran Canaria has produced a number of well-known writers, including Tomás Morales (1884–1921) and Benito Pérez Galdós (1843–1920), who were both born and bred on Gran Canaria, their works are not available in English. The Casa Museo de Tomás Morales in Moya and the Casa Museo Pérez Galdós in Las Palmas, are both open to the public and well worth a visit.

▶ **Landscapes of Gran Canaria** – Noel Rochford takes readers on a trip round the island. This guidebook includes 4 car tours, 50 long and short walks and 30 suggestions as to where to picnic.

▶ **Moby Dick** – some of the scenes in the 1956 film adaptation of Herman Melville's novel were filmed on Las Canteras beach in Las Palmas. Directed by John Huston, the cast included Gregory Peck, Richard Basehart and Leo Genn.

▶ **The History of the Discovery and Conquest of the Canary Islands** – by Juan de Abreu Galindo. Translated from a Spanish manuscript found on one of the island, this contemporary account of the mysterious pre-Spanish Canary Islands provides an interesting insight into the life of the ancient inhabitants. A difficult but rewarding read.

▶ **SOS Pacific** – This British drama film from 1959 starring Richard Attenborough and Pier Angeli was filmed on and around Gran Canaria.

on the grounds of the dreamy picnic area and there are plenty of possibilities for taking a long hike through the thickly wooded mountain landscape. *17km (11mi)*

### ROQUE BENTAIGA (129 E5) (ℳ D 4)

The majestic basalt monolith southwest of Tejeda is 1412m (4632ft) high. The first Canarians considered it sacred and sacrificial ceremonies were once held at the place of worship that can be reached from the parking area.

Traces of sites sacred to the former inhabitants have also be found in the *Cueva del Rey* (King's Cave) which is very close as the crow flies, but rather difficult to reach. At 11m long, 7m wide and with a height of 2.5m, the cave is unusually large and very impressive. *7km (5mi)*

### ROQUE NUBLO ★ (129 F6) (ℳ E 4)

Gran Canaria's most famous landmark soars into the sky like a giant's axe. The 1813m (5948m)-high 'Cloud Rock', a block of basalt, rises 80m above a flat-topped mountain. As was the case with Roque Bentaiga, the first Canarians also thought of this as a sacred place. It can be reached after about 30 minutes by following a winding path from the car park (approach from Ayacata).

Two ⠵ plateaus open up glorious panoramic views over large sections of the island as far as Tenerife. Also take a look at Roque Nublo's two companions, *Fraile* and *Rana*. Depending on where you are, with a little bit of imagination you will actually be able to recognise the profile of a monk (Spanish: *fraile*) and a frog (Spanish: *rana*) in the rocks.

If you drive further uphill, you will reach one of the Canarios' favourite picnic areas in the *Llanos de la Pez* after just a few minutes. The barbecues and picnic tables are always full at weekends; the locals like to come here with their families and

Roque Nublo: a natural stone skyscraper

relax in the beautiful landscape. This is a perfect opportunity for sociable tourists to get to know the Canarios. A few yards further on, you will see something unusual for this degree of latitude: pear and apple plantations. *14km (9mi)*

# THE NORTH

**You'll be tempted to pinch yourself and ask if you're still on the same island from where you set out less than one hour ago. No bare rocks, no arid ground. Here the sun even has a hard time breaking through the clouds and mist.**

Your first encounter with the trade winds will probably occur shortly after you leave Las Palmas behind you. They blow in towards the *cumbre* where they get caught and go no further. The result is that the ground never completely dries out and vegetation flourishes. The mild climate is perfect for farming. There are fields wherever you look: avocados, citrus fruit, medlars, guavas and lots of bananas.

You will also see the urban sprawl. Settlements have spread out wherever there is space. There are hardly any beaches; the ocean batters the rocky coastline and the white surf surges all down the coast. The *barrancos* are less majestic than in the barren south. Beehives are placed on small plateaus in the foothills and pigeons are reared. Wherever possible, there is a terraced field where people go about their work with the utmost care: planting seedlings, harvesting potatoes, hoeing. It seems like this is how it has always been. With the exception of Telde and Arucas, the only places where you will have the feeling of town life is in Gáldar and Guía that

Photo: Terraced fields in the mountains

Green hills and a rocky coastline – with terraced fields, banana plantations and lively towns in between

have now almost developed into a single built-up area, separated only by the motorway. As soon as you leave Agaete at the latest, all traces of urban life disappear. If you drive to the south along the 40km (25mi) twisting road to La Aldea de San Nicolás, the hostile environment of the steep coast will soon make you believe that you are in a completely different world.

# ARUCAS

(130 B–C2) *(⊞ F 2)* ★ **Gran Canaria's third largest town (pop. 34,000) is the home of Canarian rum.**

It is called *Arehucas* after a settlement of the first Canarians that was once located here. Enormous quantities of sugar cane started to be grown on the north slopes of the *cumbre* with its plentiful water resources in the 16th century and distilleries were soon established. A large percentage of the endemic laurel tree forests was felled so that the area could be cultivated. At the end of the 19th century, there was a boom in the banana business and Arucas became a prosperous place. You will be able to see this in the well-preserved Old Town with its two-storey houses lining the steep streets.

## CASA DE CULTURA

On your stroll along the pedestrianised street Calle León y Castillo, it is worth taking a look at the traditional architecture with the carved wooden galleries and the old, widely branching, dragon tree in the House of Culture. Sometimes there are art exhibitions; the library is always open. *Mon–Fri 9am–1.30pm and 5–8pm, Sat 9am–1pm | admission free | Calle León y Castillo 5–6*

Gothic looking: the cathedral in Arucas was actually built in the 20th century

## SIGHTSEEING

### AREHUCAS ●

The rum factory is one of the economic mainstays of the town. In started operating in 1884 and the spirits produced by the large distillery (it also makes banana liqueur) soon became famous throughout Spain. The tour of the factory also includes the bodega where famous visitors have left their signatures on the rum barrels. *Mon–Fri 9am–1.30pm | Era de San Pedro 2 | www.arehucas.com*

### IGLESIA DE SAN JUAN BAUTISTA

The Church of St John the Baptist is as big as a cathedral. From a distance, it looks like a masterpiece of Gothic architecture but it was actually built in the 20th century. The large rose window above the main portal and the reclining figure of Christ by the sculptor Manuel Ramos are especially noteworthy. *Usually only open during mass*

### JARDÍN DE LA MARQUESA

This park with plants from all over the world is owned by the Countess of Arucas.

It is also known as the *Jardín de las Hespé-rides*. *Mon–Fri 9am–noon and 2pm–6pm, Sat 10am–2pm | entrance fee 6 euros | www.jardindelamarquesa.com | GC 330 towards Bañaderos, 1km (½mi)*

### MONTAÑA DE ARUCAS ☆

The road spirals its way around the hill in the town, rising to a good 400m (1300ft). When you reach the top, you will have a fine view in all directions including a panorama of the dark-green banana plantations, some of which are covered with plastic sheeting. *1km (½mi)*

### PARQUE MUNICIPAL ●

While you have to pay to get into the Jardín de la Marquesa, a stroll through the municipal park is free. Here, strelitzias and bougainvillea, hibiscus and other gloriously coloured exotic plants flourish is lavish profusion. They are all irrigated by a sophisticated system of canals, reminding visitors of Arucas' abundant supply of water. There is a romantic building on the border of the park where works by Canarian artists are exhibited *(Museo Municipal | Mon–Fri 10am–8pm, Sat 10am–1pm | Plaza de la Constitución 2).*

### HACIENDA DEL BUEN SUCESO

The finca in a banana plantation has been painstakingly renovated. Several terraces, garden, fitness centre and pool. Excellent cooking. *18 rooms | approach: GC 330 towards Bañaderos, 1.5km (1mi) | tel. 9 28 62 29 45 | www.haciendabuensuceso.com | Expensive*

### INFORMACIÓN TURÍSTICA

*Calle León y Castillo 10 (in the Old Town)*

### FIRGAS

**(130 B2) (🕮 E–F 2)**

This small town (pop. 7000) is much more famous than Arucas. If you order a bottle of *Firgas*, you will be served excellent mineral water with a few bubbles *(con gas)* or non-carbonated *(sin gas)*. Water is everywhere you look in the village. Fountains splash and a terraced watercourse has been laid out. It is worth making a stroll around *Plaza San Roque* with the pretty church in the village centre. On your way, you will come across a mill from 1512 that is now the home of the tourist information centre *(Calle El Molino 12 | tel. 9 28 61 67 47).*

## MARCO POLO HIGHLIGHTS

### ★ Museo y Parque Arqueológico Cueva Pintada

The 'painted cave' is the most important testimony to the first people who lived on the Canary Islands → p. 63

### ★ Caldera de Bandama

Gran Canaria's largest crater is evidence of the island's volcanic origins → p. 67

### ★ Cenobio de Valerón

Spectacular group of caves with 298 chambers covering an entire wall → p. 68

### ★ Teror

A place of pilgrimage and 'typically Canarian' → p. 71

### ★ Arucas

Delightful little place with a well-preserved Old Town → p. 59

You can spend the night in rustic surroundings high up on the hill above the town. *Fonda (10 rooms | Montaña de Firgas 1 | tel. 9 28 62 55 96 | Moderate)* is a fortress-like average standard hotel with a panoramic view to the north. If you don't feel like spending so much money, you can stay in a four-bed room in the neighbouring inn, which is also quite charming *(Albergue | 12 rooms | Budget)*. Both guesthouses make good starting points for hikes and trips to the verdant gorges in the area. *7km (4mi)*

## MOYA (130 A–B2) *(𝄇 E 2)*

This village (pop. 3000), beautifully located in the foothills of the *cumbre* is famous as the home of the poet and doctor Tomás Morales (1884–1921). The house he was born in is now a museum with many personal mementos *(Casa Museo Tomás Morales | Mon–Fri 9am–8pm, Sat/Sun 10am–2pm | free admission | main street)*. The main street leads to *Plaza Tomás Morales* and the massive parish church, *Iglesia del Pilar. 6km (3¾mi)*

## PARQUE NATURAL DE LOS TILOS ☺ (130 A3) *(𝄇 E 2)*

Gran Canaria's ecological museum lies hidden away in the temperate *Monte Verde* region. Los Tilos provides an overview of the island's former vegetation. Remnants of a Canarian laurel tree forest can be found at the bottom of the shady valley INSIDER TIP *Barranco del Laurel* – dark-green trees, close together, protected from the sun and heat by the mountains. The proliferation of blackberry bushes, rushes and reeds is unbelievably dense. Ferns feel at home here, moss thrives on walls and the slopes are covered with colourful mountain flowers. There can be almost 40 inches of rainfall a year here. A narrow lane (GC 704) makes its way through the valley to the mountains. *8km (5mi)*

# GÁLDAR

**(129 E 1–2) *(𝄇 D 1)* This small town (pop. 23,000) spreads around the base of the conical volcano Pico de Gáldar.**

Casa Museo Tomás Morales in Moya traces the poet's life

Gáldar can be rather hectic even though there is a little less traffic now that the bypass has been completed. Take a stroll along the pedestrianised Calle Capitán Quesada to the *Plaza de Santiago*, one of the most picturesque squares in the Canaries, with the impressive pilgrimage church *Iglesia de Santiago*. The wide square, shaded by conifers, is full of life all day long. Gáldar has a long history. One of the two island kings resided here before the Spaniards arrived. Tenesor Semidan surrendered and allowed himself to be baptised.

## SIGHTSEEING

### EL DRAGO

Gáldar has the oldest dragon tree on Gran Canaria. The magnificent specimen was planted in 1718 and its enormously thick trunk is now almost too wide for the arcaded patio of the *Casa Consistorial*. Visits usually only possible when the tourist office in the town hall is open on workdays until 1pm | Plaza de Santiago 1

### IGLESIA DE SANTIAGO DE LOS CABALLEROS

Gáldar's main church from the early Classicist period in the 18th century, towers up behind Plaza de Santiago. The sober interior contrasts with the valuable church treasures that are displayed in the church itself as well as in the crypt. *Irregular opening hours*

### MUSEO ANTONIO PADRÓN

The former home of the artist (1920–1968) in the centre of Gáldar shows a collection of his expressionist paintings and sculptures. They hark back to an archaic, imaginary world untouched by tourism. *Entrance fee 3 euros | Mon–Fri 9am–2pm | Calle Drago 2 | www.antonio padron.com*

### MUSEO Y PARQUE ARQUEOLÓGICO CUEVA PINTADA ★

The archaeological park makes it possible to visit the famous 'painted cave', whose colourful geometric wall paintings are the most impressive witness to the island's first inhabitants, for the first time. The cave is the main attraction of a partly excavated, partly reconstructed, settlement with dozens of circular buildings. You can go into some and get an idea of how the native Canarian population once lived. Background information in several languages is provided by the multimedia stations. Finds that were uncovered during excavation work are exhibited in the museum: small idols, clay seals, jewellery and tools. You can buy arts and crafts inspired by old-Canarian artefacts in the museum shop: jewellery, ceramics, textiles and woven goods. *Tue–Sat 9.30am–8pm, Sun 11am–8pm; admission until 5pm, regular tours in English | entrance fee 6 euros | Calle Audiencia 2 | www.cuevapintada.org*

## FOOD & DRINK

### ALCORI

The cosy, rustic restaurant on the pedestrianised street near the Plaza offers an inexpensive set lunch and you can sit outside on the terrace. *Closed Sun | Calle Capitán Quesada 6 | tel. 9 28 88 36 74 | Moderate*

### CA' JUANCRI

Popular and typical bar in an old townhouse with high ceilings and ham hanging over the counter. Also, a good place for tapas. *Open daily | Calle Tagoror 1 (near the town hall) | Budget*

## INFORMATION

### INFORMACIÓN TURÍSTICA

*Calle Tagoror 3 (in the town hall) | tel. 9 28 89 58 55 | www.galdar.es*

## WHERE TO GO

### CUEVA DE LAS CRUCES
**(129 D2)** *(∅ D 2)*
Crosses carved out of stone were found in the Cave of the Crosses. Whether this was the work of missionaries trying to fight heathen customs or not, is not known. *GC 293, 2km (1¼mi) beyond Gáldar*

### SARDINA DEL NORTE ॐ
**(129 D1)** *(∅ C 1)*
This fishing village (pop. 1000) is located at the most north-westerly point of the rugged coastline. The road down to it starts at the roundabout behind the bridge at the end of Gáldar. Sardina is only busy at weekends when many Canarios come here to eat in one of the fish restaurants such as **INSIDER TIP** *La Fragata (Closed Wed | tel. 9 28 88 32 69 | Expensive)* at the end of the harbour wall; this traditional restaurant is famous for its fresh fish and seafood. 10km (6¼mi)

# PUERTO DE LAS NIEVES

**(128 C3)** *(∅ C 2)* **The lively fishing village (pop. 1000) has a wide promenade and excellent fish restaurants, craft shops and galleries.**
The catamarans operated by *Fred. Olsen (www.fredolsen.es)* depart several times a day for Tenerife from the massive harbour wall *(travel time 1 hour | return fare around 269 euros for 2 people and 1 car).*

## SIGHTSEEING

### VIRGEN DE LAS NIEVES
Unpretentious chapel with a wooden ceiling and valuable 16th-century triptych by the Flemish artist Joos van Cleve.

## FOOD & DRINK

### CASA DEL MAR ●
There is an excellent selection of fish in the 'Sea House' and that almost makes up for the fact that the view of the car park from the terrace is not exactly inspiring. The menu includes fried squid and sea snails *(lapas)*, shark steak *(filete de tiburón)* and paper-thin slices of boiled octopus *(pulpo a la gallega)*. Señor Orlando also serves miniature Gran Canaria shrimp *(quisquillas)*. *Closed Mon | Calle Nuestra Señora de las Nieves s/n (on the new quay) | Moderate*

### DEDO DE DIOS ॐ
Canarian specialties served in a large winter garden with a view of the ocean. *Closed Tue | on the harbour wall | tel. 9 28 89 80 00 | Moderate*

## WHERE TO STAY

### PUERTO DE LAS NIEVES
This charming, family-run hotel is the perfect place for a holiday away from the

Valle de Agaete: a fertile valley and the perfect place for a hike

crowds – with very good food and spa facilities. *30 rooms | Avda. Alcalde José de Armas | tel. 928 88 62 56 | www.puerto delasnieves.es | Moderate*

## INFORMATION

INFORMACIÓN TURÍSTICA
*Calle Nuestra Señora de las Nieves 1 (on the old quay) | tel. 928 55 43 82*

## WHERE TO GO

AGAETE
(129 D3) (*Ø C–D 2*)
Agaete is a pretty little town (population 6000) at the end of a fertile, sunny valley. Small streets start from the shady plaza opposite the church and wind through a labyrinth of tightly packed houses. Its somewhat isolated location has resulted in this quiet town still being very much characterised by rural life. Mónica Herrera has three, lovingly decorated, cosy rooms in the old village house **INSIDER TIP** *Casa Luna*. The professional chef serves delicious meals made of organic products if her guests wish. Patio and rooftop terrace *(Calle Guayarmina 42 | tel. 928 55 44 81 | www.ecoturismo-canarias.com | Budget)*. The four-star hotel *Roca Negra*, high up on a cliff overlooking the sea, is a comfortable place for an overnight stay; it has spacious rooms and an elegant spa *(87 rooms | El Turmán | tel. 928 89 80 09 | www.hotel-rocanegragrancanaria.com | Expensive)*. 1km (½mi)

VALLE DE AGAETE ✵
(129 D3) (*Ø D 2*)
The tranquil valley cuts 7km (4½mi) inland. It begins directly beyond Agaete and is only partially used for agriculture. You can climb up the narrow tracks in the Tamadaba Forest and go on wonderful hikes. If you fancy a stay in a romantic country house, you should book into **INSIDER TIP** *Finca Las Longueras (10 rooms | tel. 928 89 81 45 | www.laslongueras.com | Moderate)*, a large farm in the middle of the valley.

# SANTA BRÍGIDA

**(130 C4) (*F–G 3*) The shady avenues, luxuriant gardens and mountain slopes make this small town with a population of 10,000 at an altitude of around 500m (1600ft) especially attractive.**

Venerable multi-storeyed houses more than one-hundred-year-old make visitors aware that, at the end of the 19th century, Santa Brígida had already become a popular health resort for wealthy North Europeans. That is when the first hotels were opened and the well-to-do spent the winter in the mild climate of the *cumbre* or escaped here from the stifling summer heat in Las Palmas. Today, little has changed. People with enough money still live in Santa Brígida and travel to work in the capital every morning.

## FOOD & DRINK

### GRUTAS DE ARTILES

The restaurant with the best traditional cooking on Gran Canaria is far away off the beaten track. Here, almost all of the typical Canarian dishes are still prepared using recipes that have been handed down for generations – washed down with Del Monte wine. The restaurant has a large dining room and several smaller ones in caves cut into a solidified stream of lava. As the restaurant is mainly frequented by Canarios, it is usually fairly quiet during the week when you will be able to explore the grottos at your leisure. *Open daily | Ctra. Las Meleguinas GC 320 | tel. 9 28 64 05 75 | www.lasgrutasdeartiles. com | Moderate–Expensive*

### SATAUTEY

Top chefs from all over Spain present their latest creations based on delicious traditional Canarian recipes in this hotel restaurant. *Open daily | Calle Real de Coello 2 | tel. 9 28 35 53 00 | Expensive*

## WHERE TO STAY

### HOTEL SANTA BRÍGIDA

One of the last traditional hotels on the island is actually located in the Monte Lentiscal district but has been considered to belong to Santa Brígida since it opened more than 100 years ago. The renovated building with modern rooms is part of a hotel training college. Spacious garden

# CHEESE WITH A 'SHOT'

Guía is a name that makes connoisseurs' mouths water. It is one of the most flavoursome cheeses produced on the Canary Islands and it has often been awarded prizes for its outstanding taste. The secret is the mixture of milk from cows, sheep and goats and – to make it perfect – a shot of juice from the flower of the wild artichoke that makes it the *queso de flor*, the 'flower cheese'. The four-to-six-pound wheels of cheese are stored in caves to mature. There are three degrees of ripeness: after about one month the cheese is *tierno* (soft); it then develops into *semicurado* (medium) and finally *curado* (hard). Curado cheese is matured for at least ten months and tastes rather like Parmesan.

View of the Caldera de Bandama, the largest crater on the island

with old trees and pool. *42 rooms | Calle Real de Coello 2 | tel. 9 28 01 04 00 | www. hecansa.com | Moderate*

**INSIDER TIP VILLA DEL MONTE**

Seven lovingly decorated rooms in a somewhat labyrinthine country house. Informal atmosphere. The suite with its own sun terrace is spectacular. Bicycles to rent together with a repair workshop and excellent information for tours. *Calle Castaño Bajo 9 | tel. 9 28 64 43 89 | www. canary-bike.com | Budget*

## WHERE TO GO

### CALDERA DE BANDAMA/PICO DE BANDAMA ☆ (131 D4) (*ØØ G 3*)

The most beautiful panoramic view over the north of the island and Las Palmas is from the 574m (1882ft)-high Pico de

Bandama. It borders the ★ *Caldera de Bandama*, the crater of an extinct volcano. The crater has a diameter of 1000m (3280ft) and is the largest on Gran Canaria. There is a small farm 200m down at the bottom and you can hike to it over the crumbly lava stones in a good hour – but remember, the entrance at the top closes at 5pm! *7km (4½mi)*

### EL MONTE (131 D4) (*ØØ G 3*)

The oldest vineyard on Gran Canaria lies hidden behind thick walls below the Monte Lentiscal district. The grapes are still harvested by hand and processed using ancient machines. The year's vintage of *Del Monte* is sold in a flash but you might still be able to buy a bottle or two. The ☺ **INSIDER TIP** *Bodega San Juan* usually has *tinto* (red wine), *blanco* (white wine) and *moscatel* (dessert wine) to sell to its customers at prices ranging from 8–12 euros a bottle until the beginning of the following year. 😊 The winegrower does not have an official 'organic product' seal but his wines are made without the use of any insecticides. *(Mon–Sat 10am–6pm | Ctra. Monte Lentiscal–Bandama 68). 5km (3mi)*

### TAFIRA ALTA (131 D4) (*∅ G 3*)
Several suburbs run into each other on the road leading out of Las Palmas. The nicest is Tafira Alta where the vegetation in the villa gardens is especially luxuriant. A twisty road to the left will take you down to the old centre. *7km (4½mi)*

# SANTA MARÍA DE GUÍA

(129 E2) (*∅ D–E 1*) **Guía – no Canario calls the town (pop. 15,000) by its full name – is an important centre for wooden artefacts and crafts.**
*Cuchillos canarios,* the sharp Canarian knives with their fine inlaid handles, and all kinds of wood carvings are specialities of Guía. And, of course, *queso de flor* the best cheese made on the Canaries. Almost all the Old Town is a listed historical site. In 1526, Guía became independent from Gáldar – until then it had been the district where the well-off lived. Today, there are still many impressive patricians' houses on *Calle Marqués del Muni.*

## SIGHTSEEING

### IGLESIA DE LA ASUNCIÓN
The 18th-century church is on the plaza. The most interesting features in the interior are the statue of Christ on the main altar and several figures of the Virgin. These are works by the greatest Canarian sculptor Luján Pérez (1756–1815). *The church is usually only open during mass*

## SHOPPING

### QUESO DE FLOR
This is something you should not miss. This speciality from Guía is stacked up high in the cheese shops along the main street that is now closed to traffic. This is also a perfect souvenir to take home with you. One of the best addresses for cheese, as well as arts and crafts, is *La Quesera (closed Sun | Médico Estévez 3)*. The 'flower cheese' tastes even better with a glass of good wine. Try this in Carmelo Suárez' ● **INSIDER TIP** *Bar El 7*; his family makes the *queso de flor* too *(daily 9am–1pm and 4pm–8pm | Calle Marqués del Muni 45).*

## WHERE TO STAY

### HACIENDA DE ANZO
Renovated old country house in colonial Canarian style. Large garden, pool. *6 rooms | Valle de Anzo | tel. 9 28 55 16 55 | www.haciendadeanzo.com | Moderate*

## WHERE TO GO

### CENOBIO DE VALERÓN ★
(129 E2) (*∅ E 2*)
Cenobio de Valerón is the most impressive ensemble of caves used by the first people on Gran Canaria. They painstakingly chiselled 298 niches and chambers out of the soft tuff stone. The caves seem to be stuck like swallows' nest in a kind of dome that is open to the north. For a long time it was thought that these were the cells of a convent (Spanish: *cenobio*) for young women preparing for to become nuns. It now seems to be certain that this tale was simply made up, and that the first Canarians really used this labyrinth of caves for storing grain. The best time

Telde: even in the second largest town on the island, people still find time for a chat

for a visit is early in the morning. *Tue–Sun 10am–5pm | entrance fee 2.50 euros | GC 291, exit Guía/Moya, to the left through the tunnel and then towards Cuesta de Silva at the roundabout. 5km (3mi)*

# TELDE

(131 E5) (*H 4*) **The modern section of the second largest town on Gran Canaria (pop. 100,000) is hardly a feast for the eyes. However, the reduced-traffic areas**

---

> **CITY WHERE TO START?**
> **Plaza de San Juan:** It is easy to explore the historical San Francisco and San Juan districts starting from the square in front of the church. As it is difficult to find a place to park in one of the side streets, a good alternative is to leave your car on the western edge of the town and walk the 10–15 minutes to the historical centre.

---

**San Juan and San Francisco in the old part of Telde are definitely worth a visit.**
Coming from the motorway, keep right at the second roundabout for the *San Juan* district. The remains of the once attractive old city are centred around the San Juan Bautista Basilica. A lovely crib is placed on INSIDER TIP *Plaza de San Gregorio* every year at Christmas.

## SIGHTSEEING

### CASA MUSEO LEÓN Y CASTILLO
This ancient city palace is the birthplace of the León y Castillo brothers. Fernando was Spain's foreign minister from 1881 and his brother Juan worked as an architect and engineer. *Mon–Fri 8am–8pm, Sat, Sun 10am–1pm | free admission | Calle León y Castillo 45*

### IGLESIA SAN JUAN BAUTISTA
The most important church in Telde on the plaza still has its pre-1520 Gothic façade. The bell towers made of dark basalt blocks were added in the 20th century. The figure of Christ made of maize pulp that came

from Mexico in the 16th century is a real curiosity. *Usually only open during mass*

## PLAZA SAN JUAN

The asymmetric square is an excellent example of 16th-century colonial architecture bordered by white buildings with the typical wide-framed portals.

### INSIDER TIP SAN FRANCISCO

A stroll through the captivating San Francisco district is like a journey through time. Low, whitewashed houses and tiny squares lie hidden along the narrow cobblestone streets opposite Plaza San Juan. To reach them, turn right off *Calle Juan Carlos* through a narrow archway. The centre is sunny *Plaza San Francisco* with the church of the same name. There is a ❀ wonderful view of the fertile *Barranco de San Miguel* from the balustrade.

## SHOPPING

### TELAR SAN FRANCISCO ☺

Nilia Bañares Baudet's small weaving mill is next to *San Francisco Church* in the district of the same name. She dyes her jackets and blankets exclusively with plant extracts she has produced herself. *Appointments advisable: tel. 928 69 12 28*

## BEACH

The 400m (1300ft)-long beach of dark sand, the *Playa de Melenara*, is in a small bay protected from the currents by rocks. It is packed with local families at weekends. There is a wide promenade, a playground for children, green areas, snack bars and fish restaurants including *Playamar (closed Mon | Budget)* to take care of all your creature comforts. *Motorway exit Melenara, then straight ahead to the beach*

## INFORMATION

### CENTRO MUNICIPAL DE ARTESANÍA Y TURISMO

Information office with an exhibition of arts and crafts, and a shop. *Calle Juan Carlos 2 (near Plaza San Juan) | tel. 928 01 33 31*

# LOW BUDGET

▶ An overnight stay in a dormitory in the *Albergue Juvenil* in Guía only costs 6 euros per person. *Avenida de la Juventud | tel. 928 55 11 41 (Mon–Fri 9am–2pm) | www.santa mariadeguia.es/turism.htm*

▶ The spicy sausage spread *(chorizo de Teror)* that you can buy at the Sunday market in Teror and in most supermarkets is delicious on fresh aniseed rolls *(panecillo con matalauva)*.

## WHERE TO GO

### CUATRO PUERTAS
### (131 E6) (𝑚 H 4)

The rather non-descript 'Mountain of Four Gates' south of Telde was once a cult site used by the original Canarians. It has four massive rectangular entrances as well as sacrificial altars and a congregating area. There are caves where people used to live and rock drawings at the back. *GC 100 towards Ingenio | 5km (3mi)*

### VALSEQUILLO ❀
### (130 B5) (𝑚 F–G 4)

Valsequillo is the centre of the Canarian dairy industry. The town is surrounded by some of the loveliest groves of almond

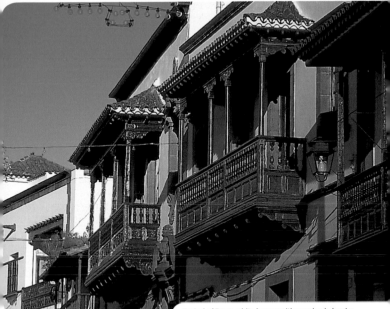

Typical of Teror: white houses with wooden balconies

trees on the island and the valley is transformed into a sea of white blossom in Feb. Starting in May, the branches are laden down with light-brown almonds. The road is also lined with fig trees and – as long as they are not on private property – you can pick the ripe fruit in autumn. *11km (7mi)*

# TEROR

(130 B–C 3–4) *(㎜ F 3)* ★ ● **If there was a title for the 'most Canarian' place of all, the town of Teror (pop. 12,000), at an altitude of 540m (1770ft) in the northern *cumbre* region, would definitely deserve it.**

Its architecture, religious importance and culinary delights – everything about Teror has a special quality. The village seems to huddle around the massive basilica,

with tranquil *Plaza del Pino* in front of it, shaded by an ancient laurel tree and surrounded by dazzling white townhouses with bleached wooden balconies and speckled roof shingles. On top of this, there are the well-preserved façades of the houses on the picturesque *Calle Real de la Plaza*. The entire Old Town of Teror is listed.

After shepherds had a vision in which the Virgin Mary appeared to them nearby on 8 September, 1481, Teror rapidly developed into the most important place of pilgrimage in the entire archipelago – and a very prosperous town. Wander slowly through the streets, admire the dragon tree on the small fenced square opposite the basilica, buy a souvenir at the ceramics stand and have a cup of coffee in one of the simple bars – you will soon see how Teror is the epitome of Canarian life.

Baroque splendour in Teror Basilica, the most important place of pilgrimage in the Canaries

## SIGHTSEEING

**BASÍLICA NUESTRA SEÑORA DEL PINO**
The Baroque building was erected between 1760 and 1767 where the pine tree used to grow, above which the Virgin Mary appeared to the shepherds in the 15th century. Only the tower of the original building remained standing after an explosion and this was integrated into the new one. The interior of the basilica is predominantly Baroque with splendidly gilded main and side altars. A cross made of the wood of the legendary pine tree is preserved under glass and is one of the church's most important relics. *Usually open during the day*

**CASA MUSEO DE LOS PATRONOS**
The small private museum is located in the former palace of the Manrique de Lara family built around 1600. The patio of the well-preserved townhouse is one of the most beautiful on Gran Canaria. The museum has exhibits of paintings, weapons and tableware from the family's estate. *Mon–Fri 11am–6pm, Sun 10am–2pm | entrance fee 3 euros | Plaza del Pino 3*

**MUSEO DIOCESANO DE ARTE SACRO**
You will have to visit the church museum behind the basilica if you want to get a close-up view of the figure of the *Virgen del Pino* seated on a throne of beaten silver. *Mon–Fri 1pm–3pm | entrance fee 1.50 euros*

## FOOD & DRINK

**BALCÓN DE ZAMORA** ↘↙
This restaurant with panoramic windows high above Teror is only crowded

at weekends. It serves delicious meat dishes. *Closed Fri | GC 21 towards Valle-seco, after 6km (3¾mi) | tel. 9 28 6180 42 | Moderate*

### CAFÉTERIA LA PLAZA

This pleasant bar is a good place to relax over a cup of tea and a biscuit after a visit to the church. *Open daily | Plaza del Pino 1 | Budget*

## SHOPPING

### SUNDAY MARKET

The Sunday market that is held around the basilica and where groceries, arts and crafts and second-hand articles are sold, is very popular with locals and tourists alike. It is also a good place to buy specialities from Teror such as the sweet nougat *turrón*. Try to get there early to avoid the traffic jams!

## WHERE TO STAY

### EL VEOR

Traditional farmhouse with three living units for two or three people in an idyllic setting only five minutes' drive from Teror. *Tel. 9 28 15 72 81 | reservations under www. ecoturismocanarias.com | Moderate*

### LA ESCALERILLA

It is only possible to reach this renovated farmhouse on a slope up a flight of steps. There is a magnificent ☆ view of the fields from the terrace. Wonderfully peaceful location. *Tel. 9 28 15 72 81 | reservations under www.ecoturismocanarias.com | Budget*

## INFORMATION

### INFORMACIÓN TURÍSTICA

*Calle Casa Huerta s/n | tel. 9 28 6138 08 | www.teror.es*

# VEGA DE SAN MATEO

**(130 B–C5)** *(⫌ F 3–4)* **The mountain village (pop. 8000) at an altitude of 850m (almost 2800ft) is much more peaceful and interesting than the wide main street and large bus station would make you think at first.**

Old townhouses along narrow, winding streets seem to be lost in their dreams. The town hall and church are located opposite each other on a small square. The locals live mainly from farming and a famous cattle market attracts visitors from all over the island on Sundays. San Mateo, as it is called, is a good place to shop for traditionally crafted wooden articles and embroidery.

## FOOD & DRINK

### 1801

You will enjoy the exquisite Canarian and Spanish cuisine served in the elegant but nevertheless countrified atmosphere of this traditional restaurant. *Closed Mon | Avenida de Tinamar 10 | tel. 9 28 66 11 26 | Expensive*

## WHERE TO STAY

### INSIDER TIP ▶ LAS CALAS ●

17th-century country estate with 9 comfortable rooms and suites, all of them individually decorated. *Lechuza area | tel. 9 28 66 14 36 | www.hotelrurallascalas.com | Moderate*

## INFORMATION

### INFORMACIÓN TURÍSTICA

*Calle Doctor Ramírez Cabrera 11 | tel. 9 28 66 13 50*

# THE SOUTH

The soil greedily swallows the water, the trickles in the *barrancos* grow into mighty torrents and raindrops bounce off the palm fronds – it is raining in the south of Gran Canaria. This only happens a few times a year and, just a short while later, everything is dry again.

The clouds brought in by the northeast trade winds seem to be stopped in their tracks in the mountains – the temperature in the south is almost always 3 to 5 degrees higher than in the north. The 350 days of sun every year turned the region into a stony desert that has to be artificially irrigated. And that means the villages on the coast that you drive past on your way to the holiday resorts seem rather bleak. Most of the tomato plantations that enjoyed bumper harvests in the 1970s have ceased to be profitable and have gone to ruin. Today, water is expensive and can be used elsewhere to greater advantage – in tourism. What used to be wasted is now recycled using the latest technology to make the flowers between the countless hotels and apartment complexes bloom.

The fantastic beaches and unique dunes in Maspalomas are the reason for hundreds of thousands of holidaymakers spending 'the best days of the year' here. Further westwards, threateningly steep cliffs rise out of the ocean. But even this area has

Photo: Playa de Maspalomas

The south attracts visitors with its sun, magnificent sandy beaches, the dunes in Maspalomas and the spectacular hinterland

been developed for tourism. No matter how small, holiday complexes have been sqeezed onto the slopes in most of the bays along the coast. A moratorium limiting the number of beds in the region was successfully dodged. Thanks to the well-oiled machinery of corruption, a surprising number of licenses supposedly issued before the agreement came to light. But now the financial crisis appears to have put a stop to the construction boom – at least, for the time being.

If you drive a short distance inland from the coast, you'll find yourself in a different world: picturesque villages and terraced fields, along with almond trees and small groves of short-trunked Canarian palm trees whose dark-green bushy crowns and orange-coloured fruit glow in the sunlight.

Rustic atmosphere with plenty of wood: the Villa de Agüimes in the former town hall

# AGÜIMES

(135 D2) *(𝑚 G 5)* **Agüimes (pop. 14,000), caught between tradition and the modern world.**

The town had grown rapidly in recent years; there is a modern swimming pool and it has its own television station. But, your footsteps echo over the cobblestones in the Old Town just as they did a hundred years ago.

## FOOD & DRINK

### OROVAL

Canarian and international cuisine using fresh ingredients – most of them, from the island. *Closed Mon | tel. 9 28 78 50 03 | Moderate*

### TASCA MI PUEBLO

Bar with rustic trimmings and a small menu of Canarian specialities. *Closed Mon | Calle Progreso 50 | tel. 6 05 80 25 61 | Moderate*

## WHERE TO STAY

### CASA DE LOS CAMELLOS

Charming country hotel with peaceful patios and inviting arcades in a 200-year-old building. *12 rooms | Calle Retama | tel. 9 28 78 50 03 | www.hecansa.com | Moderate*

### INSIDER TIP VILLA DE AGÜIMES

Attractive country hotel in the former town hall with an inner courtyard and rooms furnished in a rustic style. *6 rooms | Calle Sol 3 | tel. 9 28 78 50 03 | www.hecansa. com | Moderate*

## WHERE TO GO

### ARINAGA (135 E3) *(𝑚 H 6)*

Extensive new building has turned this former fishing village into an unsightly place. However, it is still worth taking a stroll along the sea promenade past whimsical fish sculptures. *La Farola (open daily | on the harbour wall | tel. 9 28 18 04 10 | Moderate–Expensive)* specialises in lobster. *10km (6mi)*

## GUAYADEQUE ● ☀
(134–135 C–D 1) (*m F–G 5*)

The *Barranco de Guayadeque* is one of the narrowest and steepest gorges on Gran Canaria. The sun hardly ever reaches the bottom and the *barranco* is luxuriantly green most of the year. Maybe that's the reason why the early Canarians settled here. In prehistoric times this valley was the most populated of the island. There are hundreds of cave dwellings hidden in the lava stone – many of them still lived in today. A large number of burial sites full of bones and mummified bodies from the pre-Spanish period have been discovered in Guayadeque. Information in: *Centro Interpretación (Tue–Sat 9am–5pm, Sun 10am–3pm | entrance fee 2.50 euros).*

There is a cave chapel as well as two cave restaurants in the valley. **INSIDER TIP** *El Centro (daily noon–10pm | on the left, in the middle of the valley | tel. 9 28 17 21 45 | Budget)* is made up of a series of niches and narrow, winding corridors. *Tagoror*, the large restaurant at the end of the road, is a stopping point for many tourist coaches and has a folklore show every Saturday *(daily 10am–midnight | tel. 9 28 17 20 13 | www.restaurante-tagoror.com | Moderate).* 1km (½mi)

## INGENIO
(135 D–E 1–2) (*m G 5*)

Agüime's twin had its heyday during the sugar boom when the town was dominated by the many *ingenios* (sugar mills). There is a well-preserved press at the roundabout on the road to Carrizal. Ingenio is famous as a centre for Canarian embroidery. You can buy handmade articles and other souvenirs in the *Museo de Piedras y Artesanía Canaria (Mon–Sat 10am–6pm | free admission | GC 100 at the end of the Las Mejias district).* 3km (2mi)

# ARGUINEGUÍN

(133 D6) (*m D 8*) **Today, the town that in the language of the Guanches means 'peaceful water' has a population of 12,000 and probably just as many tourists.**

The Canarios and foreigners who live here get on particularly well. Although this is a typical tourist centre, it is still possible to get a feel for everyday Canarian life. This can be found around the harbour, especially the fishing port area where old men play cards in club rooms and where fish are processed and sold in the warehouses. The

# ARGUINEGUÍN

Canarian bananas: small, mouth-watering fruit

small beach with a view of the cliff covered with palm trees has a certain charm.

## FOOD & DRINK

### COFRADÍA DE PESCADORES
The 'Fishermen's Fraternity' is located at the port next to the main warehouse where you can be quite sure that the fish is fresh! *Closed Wed | tel. 9 28 15 09 63 | Moderate*

### SU BAR
This beach restaurant, next to the cement factory (which can be seen from everywhere) in the El Pajar district, has achieved something like cult status. Juan and his crew serve paella and freshly-caught seafood at a surprising speed. *Closed Thu | Budget*

## SHOPPING

The large market where you can buy fruit, vegetables and fish, as well as arts and crafts and bric-a-brac spreads all the way from the harbour to the outskirts of Arguineguín. *(Tue 8am–2pm)*.

## WHERE TO GO

### BARRANCO DE ARGUINEGUÍN ★ ☆
**(133 D–E 2–5) (𝄞 D 5–8)**
This huge valley begins behind the banana plantations in Arguineguín. A good road takes you more than 20km (12½mi) into the mountainous world of the *cumbre*. You reach the largest reservoir on the island, the *Embalse de Soria*, surrounded by majestic palm trees and brilliantly coloured mountain flora, at a height of 900m (2950ft). The pretty restaurant *Casa Fernando (closed Sun | tel. 9 28 17 23 46 | Budget)* in the hamlet of *Soria* is an inviting place to try some tasty Canarian specialities. There are many hiking trails, but they demand a good knowledge of the area. 20km (12½mi)

### PLAYA DE LA VERGA
**(133 D5) (𝄞 C–D 8)**
This 300m-long beach is the most unusual on Gran Canaria. A property tycoon wanted to provide people living in his holiday complex with their very own beach. Ecologists rejected his proposal to take sand from the ocean bed off Gran Canaria – as was common in the past – to do this. Undaunted, he spent half a million euros to have sand shipped in from the Bahamas. Now, the bright colour of the sand gives the sea here its typical Caribbean blue colour. The best snack bar is the cheerful cafeteria *Tapas, Tapas (open daily | tel. 9 28 15 07 98 | Moderate)*. Try the delicious dates wrapped in bacon. 3km (2mi)

# LAS MELONERAS

(134 A6) *(Ⅲ E 8)* **A new resort with a promenade, shops, hotels and holiday complexes has been created here – and building has not finished yet.**

Las Meloneras is a continuation of Maspalomas to the west. The highlight: a beach 400m long of whitish sand.

## FOOD & DRINK

### LAS RIAS
Restaurant on the promenade on the upper floor of the *Varadero* shopping centre. The branch of one of Playa del Inglés' top restaurants, Rias Bajas, is the perfect place to tuck into fish and seafood on the spacious ✴ terrace with a fantastic view of the Atlantic. *Open daily | CC Varadero | tel. 9 28 14 00 62 | Moderate*

### SUNSET CAFÉ ✴
High above the CC Meloneras, with an awning to protect you from the sun, Sunset serves refreshing drinks and ice cream and offers a spectacular panoramic view free of charge. *Daily 4pm–midnight | Budget*

## SHOPPING

You can find all your heart desires in the *Varadero* shopping centre, from clothes, cosmetics and groceries to jewellery, but bargain goods are the main draw. By contrast, the arcade at the hotel *Costa Meloneras* near the beach has a splendid range of top-brand boutiques with high-quality, expensive articles. The craft market with glassblowers, portrait painters and jewellery designers, held on the Boulevard every evening, is attractive.

## SPAS

### GRAN SPA CORALLIUM ●
The spa centre in the hotel Costa Meloneras oozes the atmosphere of a luxurious Roman bath with a caldarium and frigidarium (warm and cold baths), hamam, ice grotto and a 'light-and-dream room' where you can lie on a gurgling waterbed and look up at twinkling stars while listening to the music of the spheres. The highlight is the 'Dead Sea': a spacious, artificial grotto with extremely salty water in which you can float weightlessly. *Daily 10am–8pm | day ticket: 52 euros; 45 euros for hotel guests | Calle Mar Mediterráneo 1 | tel. 9 28 12 81 81*

### THALASSO VILLA DEL CONDE
The INSIDER TIP luxurious spa in the hotel Villa del Conde is open to all. Guests are transported into an absolutely relaxing Zen-like environment. There is a seawater inhalatorium, a highly-saline gravity pool, a cold pool for Kneipp therapy treatment, as well as aromatic oil and other special showers, steam and dry saunas. *Daily*

# LOW BUDGET

▶ The cheapest accommodation in Playa del Inglés is in Residencia San Fernando. A double room will only set you back around 30 euros a night *(in San Fernando suburb | Calle La Palma 13| tel. 9 28 76 39 06).*

▶ The tasty 3-course set lunches *(menu del día)* in the simple *Los Danieles* restaurant in Puerto Rico cost about 8 euros. *Closed Sun | at the end of the CC shopping centre | tel. 9 28 56 04 15*

10am–8pm | 2½hr from 35 euros, treatments from 60 euros | Calle Mar Mediterráneo 7 | tel. 9 28 56 32 32

## ENTERTAINMENT

### CASINO
Roulette and slot machines can now also be found in Meloneras. *Daily 10am–4am, dining room from 8pm | Calle Mar Mediterráneo s/n*

## WHERE TO STAY

### BOABAB
Everything in this hotel reminds one of Africa: the fortress-like, ochre-coloured architecture, the interior design and the huge pool area with baobab trees. Even the waiters and guest hosts in their colonial-style uniforms will make you feel like you are in Africa. *677 rooms Calle Mar Adriático 1 | tel. 9 28 14 22 40 | www.lopesanhotels.com/en | Expensive*

### CAY BEACH MELONERAS
This modern, unpretentious bungalow complex is peacefully located with several attractive garden and pool areas. Ten minutes' walk to the beach. *111 units | Calle Mar Báltico s/n | tel. 9 28 14 35 97 | www.caybeach.com | Moderate*

### RIU PALACE MELONERAS
An enormous, dazzling white hotel. Generous garden areas, several pools and 144 bungalows perfectly integrated into their surroundings. *303 rooms | tel. 9 28 14 31 82 | www.riu.com | Expensive*

### VILLA DEL CONDE
The lobby looks like a church. The terrace, a plaza, and the entire complex resemble a Spanish village – a great deal of money and imagination was invested to make this an eventful, holiday idyll with gardens and pools directly on the shore. *561 rooms | Calle Mar Mediterráneo 7 | tel. 9 28 56 32 00 | www.lopesanhr.com | Budget*

# MASPALOMAS

**MAP INSIDE BACK COVER**
**(134 A6) (𝄢 E 8) This sprawling area below Playa del Inglés is bordered by the dunes, an ancient grove of palm trees and the lighthouse Faro de Maspalomas.**

Maspalomas is made even larger by several other holiday resorts further inland. The seashore promenade with cafeterias, ice cream parlours and shopping centres now stretches all the way to Las Meloneras.

## SIGHTSEEING

### DUNAS DE MASPALOMAS ★
The dunes in Maspalomas are one of Gran Canaria's most amazing natural phenomena. At their widest point, they reach almost 1.5km inland. The 1000 acres of sand with its endemic flora have been a nature

reserve since 1987. The dunes mainly consist of ground coral and shell washed up by the waves. The *dunas* are bordered to the west by the 😊 INSIDER TIP *Charca de Maspalomas*, a small lagoon of brackish and fresh water where herons, ducks, plovers, coots and many other birds stop over on their migratory flights (good information board on the promenade). Since being protected, many animals that were driven away during the construction boom have returned and are now breeding again in the reeds and rushes on the banks. Fish have also moved back and algae and grass show that the water is clean once again.

Until recently, it was possible to wander through the sandy dales with their tamarisks at will and roll out your beach towel wherever you wanted. Construction activities over the past few decades have now restricted the dunes' movement and the threat of countless visitors tramping through them led to a decision to restrict access. However, although there are a few waymarked paths through the dunes, people still go wherever they want.

## FOOD & DRINK

### CASA ANTONIO

This cosy gem with a view of the sea is tucked away in the centre of the small shopping promenade. Guests get to see the fish before it is cooked and pay for it by weight. Personal, friendly service. *Open daily | tel. 9 28 14 11 53 | Moderate*

### LA ORANGERIE

This top restaurant in the hotel Palm Beach is well known for its creative Mediterranean cuisine and good wines. *Mon, Wed, and Fri–Sat 6.30pm–10pm | Expensive*

## BEACH

### PLAYA DE MASPALOMAS

The sandy beach next to the dunes is the western extension of Playa del Inglés. There is a nudist section with sunbeds and umbrellas 2km (1¼mi) to the east. There are many restaurants and good sanitary facilities *(balneario municipal)* at the beginning of the Playa.

Water and sand: Charca de Maspalomas in front of the dunes at Maspalomas

## WHERE TO STAY

### APARTHOTEL MASPALOMAS DUNAS
The 228 flats are all in low, earth-coloured houses that have been discreetly integrated into spacious landscaped gardens. Very peaceful, with a pool but not close to the beach. *Tel. 9 28 14 09 12 | www. hotelesdunas.com | Moderate*

to the golf course. Each of the 266 split-level flats is equipped with a kitchen. Two pools, a restaurant and grocery shop. There is also a shuttle service to the beach and to Playa del Inglés. *Tel. 9 28 77 39 49 | www.cordialcanarias.com | Moderate*

### OASIS MASPALOMAS
Reasonably-priced holiday flat complex

The men in Mogán like to get together for a game of dominoes in the bar

### GRAND HOTEL RESIDENCIA ☺
This small 5-star hotel is a member of the *Leading Small Hotels of the World*. It borders on the old palm-tree oasis in Maspalomas. The 94 rooms and suites have large balconies or terraces. Excellent cuisine and an extremely environmentally conscious management. Waste water is recycled, bio-degradable cleaning agents used and plastic is avoided as much as possible. *Tel. 9 28 72 31 00 | www.seaside-hotels.de | Expensive*

### GREEN GOLF
This tranquil bungalow complex in the style of a Spanish village is located next

next to the Charca de Maspalomas and close to the beach. *91 flats | tel. 9 28 14 19 52 | www.oasismaspalomas.com | Budget*

### PALM BEACH ★
The architect Alberto Pinto transformed this house into the first design hotel on the island. The 328 rooms were pepped up with flashy colours, chrome, marble and accessories from the 1970s. The lobby, bars and restaurants celebrate this retro look. Wonderful garden, pools, spa. Close to the beach. Perfect! *Tel. 9 28 72 10 32 | www.hotel-palm-beach.com | Moderate*

# MOGÁN

(132 C2–3) (*∭ C 6*) **The coastal road stops in the southwest of Gran Canaria and turns abruptly into the mountains.**
In March, the scent of orange blossom captivates visitors to the upper section of this 12km (7½mi)-long gulch. The ⚜ *Barranco de Mogán* is the most fertile valley in the south of the island. The town itself (pop. 6000) is rather sleepy even though it is the administrative centre for the southwest.

## FOOD & DRINK

### ACAYMO
Traditional restaurant on the approach to the town with a lovely terrace and a lot of greenery. Food cooked on a charcoal grill. *Closed Mon | tel. 9 28 56 92 63 | Moderate*

### CASA ENRIQUE
One of several delightful restaurants on the main street. It specialises in hearty Canarian food made with fresh ingredients. *Open daily | Calle San José 5 | tel. 9 28 56 95 42 | Moderate*

## WHERE TO GO

**MOLINO DE VIENTO** (132 C3) (*∭ C 6*)
The landmark in Molino de Viento, a 'suburb' on the road to Puerto de Mogán that gave the village its name, has now been renovated. This impressive windmill is one of the last on Gran Canaria. *5km (3mi)*

**PAJONALES** (132 133 C–E 1–2) (*∭ D 5*)
Where the country road above Mogán turns westwards, a small lane leads straight ahead to the *Presa del las Niñas* and Ayacata. This is where the dramatically romantic landscape of Gran Canaria's largest nature reserve begins: Pajonales,

Molino de Viento's landmark

with its narrow gulches, steep mountains, expansive pine forests and a few reservoirs. Pajonales was severely damaged by forest fires in 2007 but there is hardly any trace of that today. The area is another fine example of how the Canarian pine survives fires. You can see new bright green needles growing out of the trunks wherever you look. In order to make sure that the largest single forest area in Gran Canaria recovers completely, plans are being considered to close the area – even to bikers and hikers – for a period. *3km (2mi)*

# PLAYA DEL INGLÉS

▨▨ **MAP INSIDE BACK COVER**
(134 B5–6) (*∭ E–F 8*) **This huge complex in the far south of the island is the epitome of mass tourism.**
Playa del Inglés has now almost completely fused with the neighbouring

towns of San Agustín and Maspalomas and nobody is really sure if there are beds for 100,000 or maybe even 120,000 holidaymakers in the countless bungalow and holiday flat complexes. The labyrinth of streets in 'the Englishman's Beach' makes it difficult for anybody but insiders to find their way around. Tourist officials have realised that Playa del Inglés is in urgent need of a facelift. Many new green areas have been laid out and some buildings demolished to make the holiday metropolis more attractive. Playa del Inglés offers easy access to miles and miles of beach and to the dunes – all of this with a perfect infrastructure and exuberant nightlife.

## FOOD & DRINK

### EL ASADOR CRIOLLO
Playa's top address for fans of hearty meat dishes. Mainly South-American specialities are prepared on an open grill. *Open daily | Avda. De Italia 30 (near the Mini Tren) | tel. 9 28 77 80 62 | Expensive*

### EL MUNDO
There are no borders in fusion cooking: British black pudding meets Asian apple wontons, Thai veggie-burgers team up with Greek tsatsiki. Canarios are fond of the reasonably-priced set lunches. *Open daily | Avda. De Tirajana (Edificio Tenesor) | tel. 9 28 77 61 41 | Moderate*

### INSIDER TIP ▶ LOS JOSE'S
Wide range of tapas and typical Canarian lunches in San Fernando. *Closed Sun | Calle Plácido Domingo s/n | tel. 9 28 76 96 80 | Moderate*

### RIAS BAJAS
This restaurant describes itself as a *marisquería*. The seafood and fish served in this unostentatious eatery in the Yumbo shopping centre are really exquisite! *Open daily 1pm–4pm and 7pm–midnight | Avda. De Tirajana/Avda. de EE.UU. | tel. 9 28 76 40 33 | www.riasbajas-playadelingles.com | Expensive*

# CHURROS

Many Canarios really look forward to their *churros* – thumb-thick, deep-fried pastry – at the weekend. They are definitely not for those on a diet but taste especially good after a long night on the town. Fresh out of the deep-fryer, they are dunked in thick hot chocolate. You will find *churrerías* where the locals live in Las Palmas and the San Fernando suburb of Playa del Inglés.

The miles of sand, with Playa del Inglés in the background, ends at the rocks in Maspalomas

### SAKURA III

The menu lists all of the classics of Japanese cooking: miso soup, algae salad, sushi, sashimi and various tofu dishes. The restaurant is cheerfully decorated without any frills; the show kitchen in the centre lets you keep an eye on what the sushi master is up to. If you like things more intimate, you can sit in one of the niches and eat seated on cushions on the floor. *Open daily | Avda. de Tirajana 10 | tel. 9 28 76 55 27 | www.sakura-grancanaria. com | Moderate*

## SHOPPING

### FEDAC 😊

Canarian crafts – the articles sold here are beautiful as well as useful and are made of natural materials. These include ceramic and wooden bowls, leather and palm-frond bags and even photo albums made of banana leaves. *Mon–Fri 10am–2pm and 4–7pm | Avda. De España | Yumbo shopping centre (in the Tourist Information Office) | www.fedac.org*

### MERCADO MUNICIPAL

The weekly market *(Mon–Sat 8am–2pm)* has a good range of vegetables, fruit, cheese and fish, and also lets you get a glimpse of everyday Canarian life. The flea markets *(Wed and Sat)* are also very popular.

## SPORTS & ACTIVITIES/ BEACH

### PLAYA DEL INGLÉS

This is the most famous beach on Gran Canaria and is the heart of an approximately 8km (5mi)-long 5 stretch of sand starting in San Agustín to the west and following the flowing coastline as far as the lighthouse on the Playa de Maspalomas in the far south. Access to the beach is from the *Paseo Marítimo*, an almost endless promenade that begins in the centre of the playa. There are many souvenir shops and restaurants on the *paseo*. The beach below the promenade is more than 100m wide at low tide. It is clean and light coloured and ideal for long walks. Wind shields protect sunbathers from the strong trade winds and there are kiosks every few hundred yards that sell ice cream, refreshments and snacks. The nudist beach is 2km (1¼mi) further south in the dunes. This is also where bathers seeking peace and quiet go to get away from the crowds on the main beach. On windy days, the rough waves and strong currents make the Playa del Inglés unsuitable for young children. Keep an eye out for the flags: red means that swimming is forbidden; yellow – be careful, and green – swimming is not dangerous. You can not only have fun in the water but also in the sky above. A parachute jump, in tandem with an expert, from a light plane that takes off from the airfield near San Agustín is a highlight for anyone brave enough to try it *(for bookings tel. 6 09 62 60 50 | www.skydive grancanaria.es | approx. 250 euros).*

## ENTERTAINMENT

Hundreds of restaurants, some of them with live music, do all they can to attract

Fun all night long in Playa del Inglés

customers and the cafés and bars are often open until well after midnight. The later the evening, the more the nightlife becomes concentrated in the shopping centres (CCs). The *CC Yumbo*, with its cafés, pubs and bars is also the hotspot of the gay scene. There are drag shows in *Ricky's Cabaret* and live entertainment is also offered in *Fiction* next door.

The *CC Cita* is especially popular with Germans and even the not-so-young will find what they are looking for there. The public in the *CC Kasbah* is a mixture of all sorts. There are two cult addresses for the local rock scene: the small *Relax Rock Club* has live music several times a week *(ww. relax-pub.com)* and the atmosphere in the *Turbo Rock Pub (www.turbo-rock-pub)* is also superb. However, the touts – who can become pretty pushy when trying to attract guests to the various venues – might get on your nerves.

The *CC Plaza* is right next to the *CC Kasbah*. *Pachá* is a long-running success story. It is always full and attracts the 20–40-year-old crowd. *Chic & Cream* in the centre plays dance & house after midnight and has surprising theme parties every week. Things get really lively in the disco *Nikki (Avda. de Tenerife | Apartamentos Koka)*. There is a real pilgrimage to the electro-parties in the *Ozono Club* in the Hotel Buenaventura *(Plaza de Ansite 1)* every weekend. The live-music pub *Duke's (Avda. de Tirajana 1)* has been popular for years.

## WHERE TO STAY

### CORDIAL BIARRITZ

The peaceful complex with 76 bungalows, three tennis courts (floodlit), a long pool and large playground for the kids is located in an extremely beautiful park-like setting. *Avda. de Bonn 18 | tel. 9 28 77 39 93 | www. cordialcanarias.com | Moderate*

**PARQUE TROPICAL**

Canarian-style hotel on the way into town on the sea promenade. The pool is surrounded by a garden full of palm trees and the hotel has very good sports facilities. *235 rooms | Avda. de Italia 1 | tel. 9 28 77 40 12 | www.hotelparquetropical.com | Moderate*

**RÍU PALACE**

The architecture in the style of an amphitheatre with a view of the dunes in Maspalomas has made this the most attractive hotel in Playa del Inglés. Terrace café, pool. *368 rooms | Avda. de Tirajana | tel. 9 28 76 95 00 | www.riu.com | Expensive*

INSIDER TIP **SANTA MÓNICA**

Its location directly next to the dunes is the main plus point of this complex. The 188 flats – make sure to book one on the third floor or higher so that you will have a view of the sea – are simple but practical; small garden with pool. *Paseo Costa Canaria 116 | tel. 9 28 77 24 55 | www.upartamentossantamonica.com | Budget*

## INFORMATION

**PATRONATO DE TURISMO**
*Avda. de España | CC Yumbo | tel. 9 28 77 15 50 | cit@grancanaria.com*

## WHERE TO GO

**FATAGA** ☼ (134 B2–3) (*ω E 6*)

The drive alone through this steep *barranco* north of Playa del Inglés makes an outing to Fataga a unique experience. The village itself, hidden deep in the valley, has remained an intact ensemble of shingle-roofed white houses, a small shady plaza and narrow, winding streets. A comfortable country hotel has been established on a 200-year-old farm 1km to the north. The extensive INSIDER TIP *Finca Molino*

Fataga, nestling into the slope

*del Agua* (tel. 9 28 17 20 89 | www.hotel molinodelaqua.es | *Budget)* has individually decorated rooms in its former buildings and a pool. You can dine on fine Canarian cuisine in the restaurant on the terrace *(open daily | tel. 9 28 17 22 44 | Moderate).* 15km (9mi)

**MUNDO ABORIGEN** ☼
(134 B4) (*ω E 7*)

The 'World of the Aborigines', an open-air museum dealing with the life and traditions of the first Canarians, is also located in the *Barranco de Fataga*. Copies of old round stone houses, caves, burial sites and stables have been built in the spacious grounds. Figures show everyday work and customs. Unfortunately the complex is slowly becoming dilapidated as no money is being invested in its upkeep. It can therefore only be recommended to those who are really interested in the subject. *(Daily 9am–6pm | entrance fee 10 euros | approach via San Fernando along the GC 60, then turn left. 7km (4½mi)*

### INSIDER TIP PARQUE ARQUEOLÓGICO
(134 B3) *(ш E–F 6)*
On the edge of the tiny village of Artenara deep in the *Barranco de Fataga*, you will find a path through a graveyard in a rockslide. Excellent information on the burial rites of the island's early inhabitants, as well as its flora and fauna is provided on a board. Park your car along the approach to the village and follow the path. *GC 60, turn left after 11km (7mi)*

# PUERTO DE MOGÁN

(132 B–C4) *(ш B–C 7)* ★ **Many daytrippers come from all over the island to stroll through the 'Venice of Gran Canaria' (pop. around 1000, 3000 beds).**
At the end of the 1980s, an attractive tourist resort in Andalusian-Venetian style with small white houses, narrow streets and canals leading to the sea was built in front of this tiny fishing village. Since then, shops, restaurants, a shopping centre and two new hotels have opened their doors in this valley. The new promenade is slowly coming to life and live music is often performed on the pretty plaza at the weekend. The old village itself has a picturesque location on the cliffs above the steep coastline. Fishing boats, a small boatyard and the warehouse were integrated into the port. Cars, on the other hand, have been banished from the centre of the village.

## FOOD & DRINK

### COFRADÍA DE PESCADORES
Fine fish dishes are served in elegant surroundings in the restaurant run by the local fishermen's guild off the beaten tourist track in the port – nowhere else will you get fresher fish! *Open daily | Muelle | tel. 9 28 56 53 21 | Moderate*

### INSIDER TIP LOS GUAYRES
In this restaurant, one of the top Gran Canarian chef's fusion style of cooking makes traditional Canarian dishes more sophisticated by adding a touch of international cuisine. Try the tuna carpaccio! *Closed Mon | Avda. de los Marrero | tel. 9 28 72 41 00 | Expensive*

### ORILLAS DEL MAR
This traditional restaurant is known for its simple but excellent fish dishes. At weekends, the boss Antonio Navarro and his friends often get out their guitars and sing Cuban songs for the diners. *Closed Wed | Calle Esplanada del Castillete 10 | tel. 9 28 56 53 16 | Moderate*

### INSIDER TIP QUÉ TAL
Everybody in Norway knows the television chef Stena Petterson. His small temple to culinary expertise enchants connoisseurs every evening. *Closed Sun | El Paseo de mis Padres 34 | tel. 9 28 15 14 88 | www. restaurante-quetal.com | Expensive*

## SHOPPING

### MERCADO
Things become quite chaotic in Puerto de Mogán on Fridays when tourists from all over the south flock to the market *(9am–2pm)* despite the fact that there's nothing

particularly special about it: a lot of kitsch, commerce and hardly any genuine crafts.

### VIVEROS MOGÁN

Nursery and market garden in the centre of the *barranco* of Puerto de Mogán. Lovers of subtropical plants will find just what they are looking for here – seeds are also on sale. *Mon–Fri 8am–6pm, Sat 8am–1pm | driving from Puerto Rico, turn onto the tarmac road 200m before the junction*

*1pm | tel. 9 28 56 51 08 | www.atlantida-submarine.com | at the harbour wall).*
The yacht marina *Puerto Deportivo* with moorings for 220 vessels is the most popular on Gran Canaria and specialises in trans-Atlantic yachts *(tel. 9 28 56 56 68)*. Puerto de Mogán's main beach has been completely restocked with fresh sand. The canal next to it is also cleaned regularly. The beach of fine sand is about 300m long and there are sunbeds and showers.

## SPORTS & ACTIVITIES

● The 'Yellow Submarine' run by the *Undersea* company departs from the harbour wall at the port and heads for the bottom of the Atlantic. You can watch the great variety of Gran Canaria's sea life through large portholes during the 40 minute tour *(daily 10am–5pm | 28 euros | bookings Mon–Fri 9am–1pm and 4–7pm, Sat 9am–*

## ENTERTAINMENT

A stroll at sunset is just about the most exciting thing Puerto de Mogán has to offer in the evening. Locals and tourists get together on the plaza, the *Mogán* bistro-café mixes cocktails until midnight, the *Bohemia Bar* in an old village house on Paseo los Pescadores near the canal has become a popular watering hole.

Puerto de Mogán: the somewhat different holiday resort in Andalusian-Venetian style

## WHERE TO STAY

### CASA LILA
This small guesthouse is located on the opposite side of the *barranco* to the village. It has 10 flats with accommodation ranging from a studio with a raised bed to a more spacious flat with panoramic terrace. *Tel. 9 28 56 57 29 | www.apartmentscasalila. com | Budget*

### CORDIAL MOGÁN PLAYA
Spacious complex in a luxuriant garden made even more attractive by the varied architectural styles of the pool and living areas. Relaxed atmosphere. *487 rooms | tel. 9 28 72 41 00 | www.cordialcanarias. com | Expensive*

### MOGÁN VALLE
This hotel on a slope caters especially for families. The 303 units are spacious and

have a living room, large kitchen and terrace. Three pools, excellent spa. *Tel. 9 28 56 54 22 | www.cordialcanarias.com | Moderate*

### GUESTHOUSES
There are several reasonably priced guesthouses in the village and in Lomo Quiebre on the access road including *Salvador (tel. 9 28 56 53 74) | Pensión Eva (tel. 9 28 56 52 3) | Pensión Lumy (tel. 9 28 56 53 18) | Pensión Juan Déniz (tel. 9 28 56 55 39) | all Budget*

## WHERE TO GO

**INSIDER TIP ▶ GÜIGÜÍ** ☀ ☺
**(132 A1) (Ø A 5)**
The most beautiful of all of Gran Canaria's beaches has managed to protect itself from the adverse aspects of the tourism boom. The location of *Güigüí Grande* ('big') and *Güigüí Chico* (small) on the untamed steep western coast has thwarted any plans for development and the area is now a protected nature reserve. You have to make a three-hour hike from the small village of *Tasartico* over a mountain in the blazing sun to reach the shore (can only be recommended for fit hikers armed with a map). But make sure you ask for exact directions before setting out! A cliff casts its shadow over the 300m-long Güigüí Grande; the 600m beach at Güigüí Chico follows behind a rocky ledge. The strong tides mean that it is only possible to move between them at low tide. There are no sanitary facilities and no way of getting aid in a hurry should there be an accident. If you plan to make a day trip (don't forget that you need sturdy shoes, food, water and sun protection) make sure you know the times of the tides. There are also catamaran trips to the beaches (from 50 euros) from *Puerto Rico* and *Puerto de Mogán*. *33km (20½mi)*

Twilight feeling: the promenade at Puerto de Mogán

### PLAYA DE VENEGUERA
(132 B3) (*𝖒 B 6*)

You can reach this secluded 700m-long beach of sand and shingle on foot (return hike around 5 hours, no shade) along the good private road over the mountain from the village *Lomo Quiebre* or by car (poor surface) off the road to Aldea de San Nicolás (turn to *Las Casas de Veneguera*). *24km (15mi)*

# PUERTO RICO

(132 C5) (*𝖒 C 7*) **Holiday complexes have been built, one above the other, up the steep slopes on both sides of the bay.** Puerto Rico was one of the first holiday resorts. In the early 1970s, the first flats were built where nothing had existed before. The village has expanded to include the two side valleys and now boasts around 30,000 beds. Those who know Puerto Rico well, appreciate its many positive aspects. There are fewer clouds than on the south-east coast, the bay is protected from the wind and it has excellent sports facilities. Its outstanding infrastructure makes Puerto Rico a good place for families with children.

Only for fit hikers: the track to the Güigüí beaches

*Edificio Porto Novo | tel. 9 28 56 09 01 | Expensive*

## FOOD & DRINK

**INSIDER TIP** ▶ CHURRERÍA

Every morning this simple inn serves *churros*, tasty deep-fried pastries that tastes even better with a cup of hot chocolate. *Open daily | next to the garage | tel. 9 28 56 20 21 | Budget–Moderate*

### DON QUIXOTE

The friendly, unhurried atmosphere and above-average quality of the food served make this specialist for fish and meat dishes stand out from the mass of restaurants. *Closed Sun and Mon | Puerto Base*

## SPORTS & ACTIVITIES

You can play tennis in the park in front of the shopping centre. There is a playground and trampolines and children's bungee near the bus station, as well as two crazy-golf courses in the park. The 300m beach of light-coloured sand, the *Playa del Puerto Rico*, is protected by the harbour walls and there are also sanitary facilities and cafeterias. You can try paragliding and jet skiing on the beach or just cruise around in a pedal boat. Diving is also possible. *Aquanauts Dive Centre* even offers dives at night so that you can get a look at the nocturnal underwater world *(Puerto Base | Local 5 | tel. 9 28 56 06 55 | www.aquanauts-divecenter.com)*.

## ENTERTAINMENT

If you are no longer a teenager and like draught German beer, *Oscar's Pub* on the sea promenade is the place to go. The youngish crowd lets its hair down after midnight in the shopping centre *CC*. The most popular disco pubs at the moment are: *Bora Bora, Snoopy, Piccadilly, Harley's* and *Disco Joker (all on the first floor)*.

## WHERE TO STAY

### GLORIA PALACE AMADORES 🌿

The 392-room hotel with a fantastic view of the sea is located high up above the steep coastline, 5 minutes from Playa Amadores. Sun terraces, pools, spa facilities and a special programme for children. Tip: the rooms in the upper complex are more peaceful. *Avda. La Cornisa | tel. 9 28 12 85 10 | www.hotelgloriapalace.com | Moderate*

### MARINA SUITES 🌿

This no-frills apartment hotel with a garden is located on the yacht marina. The pool is directly on top of the cliff. *216 rooms | Puerto Base s/n | tel. 9 28 15 37 18 | www.marinasuitesgrancanaria.com | Moderate*

## INFORMATION

**OFICINA DE INFORMACIÓN TURÍSTICA** *Avda. De Mogán (at the roundabout) | tel. 9 28 15 88 04 | www.mogan.es*

## WHERE TO GO

### PLAYA AMADORES
(132 C5) (*Ø C 7*)

A fantastic ⭐ 🌿 *coastal promenade* with a magnificent view of the sea connects Puerto Rico with Playa Amadores that you reach after a 15-minute walk. The 400m-long beach was stocked up using gravelly shell sand from the sea. Harbour walls protect it from high waves making it quite safe for children to swim here. There are car parks, sunbeds to rent and excellent sanitary facilities, as well as shops, ice cream parlours and restaurants. This is rounded off with a lovely golf course,

The sheltered Playa Amadores near Puerto Rico is ideal for families with children

playground, restaurants and the ● ⚜ **INSIDER TIP** *Amadores Beach Club (open daily | tel. 9 28 56 00 56 | www.amadores beachclub.com | Moderate)* at the northern end. The elegant glass pavilion has a restaurant, a snack bar, chill-out lounge and a private area with sunbeds. ⚜ *Gloria Palace Hotel (tel. 9 28 12 86 40 | www.gloriapalaceth.com | Moderate)* high above the bay has wonderful panoramic views – from the 238 rooms, the sun terrace and the main pool. A second pool is completely glassed in. *Mirador del Atlantico* with 116 flats and a sea view is ideal for a self-catering holiday *(tel. 9 28 15 30 53 | www.miradordelatlantico.com | Moderate)*. *1km (½mi)*

## PLAYA DEL CURA (132 C5) *(𝄞 C 7)*

Narrow, 300m-long sandy beach with a small promenade. Peaceful atmosphere, large pool with marina restaurant and bar *(open daily | Moderate)*. *8km (5mi)*

## BOAT TRIPS ●

The boats operated by ★ *Líneas Salmón* and the glass-bottomed boats run by

*Líneas Blue Bird* operate regularly between Puerto Rico and *Arguineguín* (20min) and *Puerto de Mogán* (30min). These trips ⚜ are a perfect opportunity to see Gran Canaria from the water: steep, rugged cliffs – and, unfortunately, also over-developed gorges *(daily 10am–4.30pm | return trip 10 euros | Puerto Escala and Puerto Base)*.

## TAURITO (132 C4–5) *(𝄞 C 7)*

Along the shore there is a beach of dark sand 250m long. From here, *Lago Oasis* (entrance fee 11 euros), a seawater swimming and lesure park, stretches inland. There are tennis courts and a crazy-golf course a little higher up. The *Paradise Resort* offers live music and professional dance shows on its open-air stage almost every evening. Large hotel and apartment complexes sprawl up both sides of the valley. One of the most attractive is the *LTI Valle Taurito*, built with a great deal of natural stone and wood. It organises sporting activities and also has a large indoor swimming pool *(190 rooms | tel. 9 28 56 52 63 | www.lti.de | Moderate)*. *10km (6¼mi)*

## TAURO (132 C 4–5) *(𝄞 C 7)*

The *Playa de Tauro* is the last beach not to have been completely developed for tourism in the south of Gran Canaria. The pleasantly simple inn **INSIDER TIP** *Vista Mar (open daily | Budget)* with an open terrace and good fish dishes is located on the beach of dark sand 200m long. The *Pio-Pio* next door has similar fare on the menu. *5km (3mi)*

## LAUREL TREES (132 C5) *(𝄞 C 7)*

At the end of the Puerto Rico valley, near a small settlement, there are two ancient laurel trees in which there are always hundred of birds twittering away in the branches. *2km (1¼mi)*

# SAN AGUSTÍN

**MAP INSIDE BACK COVER**
(134 B–C5) (*F 8*) Everything is a little more relaxed and refined here than in Playa del Inglés. The sometimes extremely precipitous coastline has ensured that the terraced bungalow complexes have magnificent sea views and are protected from the trade winds.
The relatively old hotels have spacious gardens. If you choose to stay in the newer sections you will still have panoramic views but further to go to the beach.

## FOOD & DRINK

**INSIDER TIP** BAMIRA
A gastronomic experience of a special kind! The proprietors have decorated their small, tucked away, restaurant with unusual paintings and installations. The dishes also have an equally artistic touch and include scallops with sea-urchin curry and lamb fillet with palm honey. *Closed Wed | Calle Los Pinos 11 | Playa del Águila | tel. 9 28 76 76 66 | www.bamira.com | Moderate*

**INSIDER TIP** EL PUENTE
The stunning view along the lit-up coast makes this restaurant the ideal dinner location. *Tue–Sun 5.30–10.30pm | Calle Las Dalias 3 | tel. 6 79 77 10 36 | www.restauranteelpuente.com | Moderate–Expensive*

## BEACHES

*Playa de las Burras* is a 400m-long bay bordered by rocks on both sides and perfectly protected from the waves. Sunbeds and umbrellas for hire but there are no sanitary facilities. *Playa de San Agustín* is an almost 900m-long beach of fine sand with only a few rocks here and there. It is bordered by steep cliffs on both sides that separate it from the Playa de las Burras to the west. The unspoiled beach of dark sand starts in a small bay and is up to 100m wide. No WCs or showers.

## SPAS

### TALASOTERAPIA CANARIAS ●
The 2½ acres spa and health centre is located next to the Hotel Gloria Palace. Three pools, dozens of therapy facilities, trained staff and a fitness centre make this the top address in the Canaries. *Las Margaritas s/n San Augustín | tel. 9 28 76 56 89 | www.hotelgloriaplace.com*

## ENTERTAINMENT

### CASINO
Roulette, blackjack and one-armed bandits. You should be smartly dressed and have an identity card/passport with you. A spectacular, two-hour dance show is held in the same building *(Tue–Sat from 10pm |*

San Agustín's sea promenade

*entrance fee 50 euros). Daily 8pm–4am | entrance fee 3 euros | Hotel Melía Tamarindos | Calle Retama 3*

## WHERE TO STAY

### IFA INTERCLUB ATLANTIC

This holiday complex with a large pool area, waterfalls, islands, bridges, whirlpools and a gigantic garden and park caters especially to families with children. Comprehensive sports and games programme, diving school on the premises. *408 flats | Calle Los Jazmines 2 | tel. 9 28 77 02 00 | www.ifahotels.com | Moderate*

### MELÍA TAMARINDOS

One of the two traditional hotels in San Agustín. The extensive garden has direct access to the beach. One of only two casinos in the south of the island is in the basement. *279 rooms | Calle Retama 3 | tel. 9 28 77 40 90 | www.solmelia.com | Moderate*

## WHERE TO GO

### BAHÍA FELIZ (134 C5) (*ꕔ F 8*)

The Moorish style architecture of this holiday complex makes it something out of the ordinary. Many of the bungalows have small towers and domes. There is only one hotel, a small shopping centre and a few restaurants, but there are several surf schools to make up for this. It is a little difficult to get to Playa del Inglés by public transport. The *Mistral* windsurfing school is on the premises. *3km (2mi)*

### GRAN KARTING CLUB (134 C5) (*ꕔ F 7*)

The Canaries' largest go-kart track – 1.6km (1mi) circuit – is located near *Tarajalillo*. There are small karts for children between 6 and 11 and a special circuit with electro-karts for the three-to-six year olds as well as a cafeteria *(daily 10am– | karts 18 euros*

The racing circuit at the Gran Karting Club

*for 8 minutes | motorway exit: Tarajalillo). 1km (½m)*

### POZO IZQUIERDO 🔄

### (135 E3) (*ꕔ H 6*)

The largest wind energy plant on the island dominates the landscape behind the surfing beach. One of the last seawater saltworks on Gran Canaria, the **INSIDER TIP** *Salina de Tenefé* with 365 salt pans, is also there. Sea salt is harvested almost entirely by making use of the wind and sun. *Take the tarmac road from Pozo Izquierdo towards the wind energy plant, pass the Instituo Tecnológico de Canarias and then follow the short track on the left towards the sea; turn left after the fence. 13km (8mi)*

### SIOUX CITY (134 C5) (*ꕔ F 7*)

Actors re-enact scenes from the Wild West between wooden houses, a bank, sheriff's office and shops that look as if they have come straight out of a film, in this *barranco* near San Agustín. These include a bank holdup, an ambush and all other kinds of action. On Friday evenings, there is a large barbecue and live music until midnight. Admission also includes drinks at those events *(Tue–Sun 10am–4pm | entrance fee 17 euros | Fri 8pm with barbecue: 50 euros | Cañon del Aguila | exit: Playa del Aguila | tel. 9 28 76 25 73). 2km (1¼mi)*

# TRIPS & TOURS

The tours are marked in green in the road atlas, the pull-out map and on the back cover

## 1 IN THE SHADOW OF 'SNOW PEAK'

🚗 This 130km (80mi) tour of the mountainous area in the south is mainly along minor roads with little traffic. You pass tranquil villages and a rustic finca with donkeys and visit the former bishop's town of Agüimes on your way to the Barranco de Guayadeque with its mass of caves. If you like, you can finish the day in a fish restaurant on the seaside promenade in Arinaga.

After you leave Playa del Inglés → p. 83 on the GC 60, drive up into the mountains by way of San Fernando and Fataga → p. 87. It is worth making a short stop near the church in San Bartolomé de Tirajana → p. 52 to see the erstwhile *gofio* mill, the Hacienda del Molino. It has now been transformed into a restaurant and you might want to have a break in the courtyard.

You turn off onto the narrow GC 654 a couple of miles after you leave the village. Holidaymakers seem to be almost completely unaware of this route even though it is one of the most beautiful in the south of the island. Small houses built of natural stone, surrounded by palms and almond trees, seem to crouch beneath gigantic rock faces. The reeds in the narrow side

Photo: Agüimes

There is much more to Gran Canaria than just sandy beaches: tours into the mountains, to picturesque villages, reservoirs and gorges

valleys are fed by springs and are sometimes as high as a house.

The first hamlet you arrive at, called **Agua-latente** ('hidden water'), is named after the water that trickles down through the rocks from the highest peaks. The small road continues in a wide circle and you will always have a view of the **Caldera de Tirajana**, a rugged eroded crater that opens up to the sea in the distance.

Later you travel past the base of the **Risco Blanco**, a weather-beaten, brightly shining gigantic monolith. When you reach the next village **Taídia**, keep your eyes open for the (virtually hidden) signpost to the ☺ **INSIDER TIP** donkey finca Burro Safari Las Tirajanas. Almost everything that is grown here is organic, even if there is no label to prove it. You can sit on one of the rustic wooden benches in the shade of the vine-covered pergola and enjoy all of the good things the Martín family have to offer: fresh cheese from the milk of their pet goats, spicy, preserved olives that they harvest themselves, and 'wrinkled potatoes' with fiery *mojo* sauces. This all goes down well with a glass of dry table wine followed by a thimble of home-made *mejunje* fruit liqueur. Teetotallers will enjoy the orange juice, freshly pressed from sun-ripened fruit that grow in the garden. There are more than 60 well-looked-after donkeys – in colours ranging from light beige to black – waiting to be ridden. Children especially will enjoy the half-hour ride along bridle paths in the mountains. For the less adventurous, there is a petting zoo with spotlessly clean pigs and rabbits, goats, sheep and ostriches *(daily 10am–4pm | from 10 euros per person | El Morisco s/n | tel. 9 28 18 05 87 | www.burrosafari.com)*.

The next village, sleepy Santa Lucía → p. 53, also deserves closer inspection. You can have a look at the mosque-like domed church, take a leisurely stroll along the street above the through road, and have a look at the old-Canarian finds in the grey-slate 'fortress', the Museo Castillo de la Fortaleza → p. 54: ceramic bowls and jars, leather aprons and baskets made of palm fibres; there are even the remains of a mummy on display.

All of these come from the gigantic fortified mountainous area La Fortaleza Grande below the village, where the last native-Canarian warriors barricaded themselves during the Spanish conquest in 1483. It is said that many of them leaped to their death from the mountain when their supplies ran out and capitulation seemed inevitable. If you stop at the viewpoint, you will be able to see the Presa de la Sorrueda reservoir, surrounded by palm trees, glittering down below. Provided you are wearing the right shoes and are not afraid of heights, you can go up the mountain and explore its cave-like overhangs. After this, drive back towards Santa Lucía and turn right onto the GC 550. The narrow twisty mountain road takes you through a harsh landscape of weathered mountain sides worn away by water and the winds. From time to time you will come across split boulders standing like giants along the side of the road. The village of Temisas on a wide mountain spur is very picturesque. Hundred of olive trees flourish on the terraces around it and, for some time now, their fruit has been used to produce outstanding oil. You should order freshly baked bread trickled with olive oil, some spicy preserved olives and young goat's cheese in the village bar opposite the tiny church (a little bit off the through road). You just have to ask for 'pan fresco con aceite de oliva de Temisas, aceitunas y queso de cabra, por favor!' and you will be served a simple but really tasty snack.

The road then continues around lots of bends through the sun-parched mountain slopes to Agüimes → p. 76 where you should take a closer look at the historical centre with its cobblestone streets that all lead to the *Iglesia de San Sebastian*, the church with the Madonna of the Rosary. A visit to the former bishop's palace that now houses the *Museo de la Historia (Tue–Sun 8.30am–1.30pm and 4pm–6pm | entrance fee 2.50 euros | Calle Juan Alvarado y Saz 42)* is also very interesting. Instead of being presented with simple historical facts, you can learn something about everyday rituals from times gone by – witchcraft included!

After all this culture, it's back to nature! The Barranco de Guayadeque → p. 77 that starts beyond Agüimes (well signposted) is a narrow gorge, flanked by high rock faces, with many springs that keep it green throughout the year. The road winds its

Caves in the rocks: the Museo de Guayadeque displays ancient Canarian artefacts

way past colossal agave plants, cacti and gigantic ferns. The small, rustic picnic places under the eucalyptus trees are an inviting spot to take a rest.

Many Canarios come here at the weekend and on public holidays. Sometimes the number of visitors has to be restricted and you might have to wait a little. The **Museo de Guayadeque** *(Tue–Sat 9am–5pm, Sun 10am–6pm),* built into the rock like a cave, is a good place to make your first stop. Archaeologists have discovered many caves in the Barranco de Guayadeque, built before the arrival of the Spanish, where the native Canarios lived and also buried their dead. Some of the finds are on display in the museum. Next to it, there are display boards with information on the flora, fauna and geology.

**Cuevas Bermejas** is a good place for you second break; starting from the chapel in the rock, you will be able to climb up over the steep wall of rock riddled with holes. When you almost reach the end of the

road, you should park your car and have a hearty Canarian meal in one of the cave restaurants. If a terrace restaurant on the seashore is more to your liking, continue to the coast at **Arinaga** → **p. 76**. The trip through the industrial area can be a bit sobering after so much natural beauty, but you will be rewarded with an attractive promenade that stretches for miles along the ocean – and you will hardly see any tourists in the fish restaurants. You can then drive back to Playa del Inglés and the other resorts in the south in no time along the GC1.

## 2 THROUGH THE WILD *CUMBRE*

This 140km (87mi) tour takes you into Gran Canaria's mountains. You should allow yourself a full day for it – the roads are narrow and extremely twisty and driving for hours can be very strenuous. But there are many places where you can stop and admire the magnificent views, relax over lunch and get to know the island from its peaceful, unspoilt side. You should not forget to take a pullover and something to keep your head warm with you as it is often chilly and nowhere nearly as sunny as on the coast!

greenery make it the most picturesque village in the southern part of the *cumbre*. There is a camel paddock just before you reach Fataga that also offers rides.

The next stop, San Bartolomé de Tirajana → p. 52, lies at an altitude of 900m (almost 3000ft). You will now see the walls of the *cumbre* rising vertically in front of you.

'Cloud Rock': the steep Roque Nublo soars up and touches the clouded sky

Leave Playa del Inglés → p. 83 and drive through San Fernando and take the GC 60 up into the mountainous *cumbre* region. The barren Barranco de Fataga → p. 87 opens up before you in varied shades of ochre. After a visit to the open-air museum Mundo Aborigen → p. 87 and the archaeological graveyard Parque Arqueológico → p. 88, continue along the winding road over ☀ a pass (view point) and down into the valley again to Fataga → p. 87. Its small white houses and luxuriant

The landscape becomes more fertile and this is where apricots and potatoes are cultivated. Shortly after Cruz Grande you reach the highest point on this tour at 1260m (4133ft) before driving over a pass into the next *barranco*. In the distance, you will be able to make out the water of the reservoir, the Embalse de Chira, glittering in the sun. The hamlet of Ayacata → p. 56 comes into sight after a short distance. Surrounded by almond trees it appears like something out of a fairy tale when they come into blossom in January and February.

After this, take the GC 600 to the northeast. After a few hairpin bends, the Roque Nublo → p. 57 suddenly appears. This 80m-high monolith can be seen from many places in the *cumbre* but its size and shape always seem to be different depending on where you are. You then drive through extensive pine forests and fruit plantations to the junction at Cueva Grande and turn right (on the GC 130) to Pico de las Nieves → p. 49. The 'Snow Peak', at an altitude of 1949m (6394ft), is the highest point on the island. It occasionally snows here in December and January and sometimes it doesn't not melt for weeks in sheltered spots.

The surfaced road to the right takes you up to the ☀ INSIDER TIP highest viewpoint – follow the fence around the military site whose domes can be seen from miles away. Stop and take some time to take in the fantastic view! The countryside is steep and rocky to the south and east, while the north and west are densely forested. In good weather, the clouds blown in by the trade winds can reach a height of 1700m (5600ft) and squeeze into the fissures of the *barrancos* and between the mountains. At the other end, the massive cone of Teide on Tenerife abruptly forces its way through the cloud cover. Spain's highest mountain soars up to an height of 3718m (12523ft).

Now drive back to the Cueva Grande junction and then straight ahead (GC 150) down to Cruz de Tejeda → p. 48. You will be able to make out Las Palmas far away in the haze. Cruz de Tejeda is a tourist hotspot in an otherwise peaceful area. All kinds of souvenirs are for sale, children can ride a donkey for a small tip and, if you really feel like it, you can have a meal in one of the restaurants. The road down to Tejeda (GC 15) passes through avenues

of eucalyptus trees. From time to time, you catch glimpses of the Roque Bentiga (1412m/4632ft) through the branches. Tejeda → p. 54, at an altitude of 1050m (3445ft), is probably the most picturesque village on Gran Canaria. Its unspoiled character, with narrow streets, flights of stairs, squares and the church that dominates the centre make it unique, and strolling around it is a delight.

Now take the GC 60 to the south. After about 4km (3mi), turn right towards Roque Bentaiga → p. 57. You can reach the sacred basalt rock on foot which has a number of grooves carved into it to hold liquids offerings. There are several cave dwellings in the rocky walls – the largest is the impressive Cueva del Rey → p. 57. Continue on this road towards Ayacata. Shortly before you reach the village take a sharp right turn onto the GC 605 to the Embalse Cueva de las Niñas → p. 56. You will get a feeling for the peace and solitude of Gran Canaria's mountainous region on this little-used road. The 'Maiden's Cave Reservoir' is definitely the most delightful on the island. Stop for a break on its shore and enjoy your picnic lunch or even pitch your tent. Many Canarian families come here at weekends to do just that!

The last stretch of the tour is more adventurous. You will need all of your driving skills to tackle the steep road into the fertile Barranco de Mogán → p. 83. Mogán → p. 83 itself is a pleasant, sleepy little village with a few bars. The trip to the coast then takes you through the loveliest valley in the south, the fruit and vegetable garden of Gran Canaria. The valley is filled with an enchanting aroma when the orange trees blossom at the end of March. Plant lovers often stop at the large nursery Viveros Mogán → p. 89 at the end of the gorge to buy souvenirs. The coastal road and motorway then take you back to your starting point in Playa del Inglés.

# SPORTS & ACTIVITIES

Water sports – from sailing and diving to surfing and sailboarding – take pride of place on the island but the Canarios also like cycling and hiking. There are tennis and squash courts as well as crazy-golf courses in all holiday resorts.

The many important sporting events held during the year include the international INSIDER TIP football tournament in Maspalomas in January when major European teams take part, the windsurfing world cup in Pozo Izquierdo in June, the Copa del Mundo bicycle race at the beginning of December and the popular open running race, Carrera San Silvestre, held in Maspalomas on the last Sunday in the year.

## BOARD SURFING

The best spots for board surfing on Gran Canaria are at the south and north ends of Las Canteras beach in Las Palmas (Cícer/ El Confital). Qualifying contests for the World Cup are held there every year.

## CLIMBING

Mountain climbing and canyoning are becoming more and more popular. The best spots are Roque Nublo and the areas around Ayacata, Tamadaba and Sorrueda. *Canariaventura (next to the bus station in Maspalomas | tel. 9 28 76 61 68 or 6 70 77*

**Sailing, surfing and diving are Gran Canarian highlights. Landlubbers will prefer cycling and hiking**

73 43 | www.canariaventura.com) organises guided tours *(e.g. half-day | two ascents | 50 euros/person | min. 4 participants)* and also provides the necessary equipment.

### CYCLING

The difference in altitude and the change in the climate make being in good shape absolutely necessary for strenuous cycling tours. The Barranco de Ayagaures, the Barranco de Arguineguín, and higher up near the Cueva de las Niñas reservoir are just three of the many superb routes for road cyclists. But remember: you have to wear a helmet! Bikes can be rented from *Happy Biking* in Playa del Inglés that also offers tours ranging from easy to difficult *(tel. 9 28 76 68 32 | Hotel Ifa Continental | Avda. Italia 2 | www.happybiking.com |*

tour incl. transfer from 45 euros). Villa del Monte in Santa Brígida, far off the beaten track, has developed into a popular meeting place where bikes can also be hired and repaired (www.canary-bike.com).

## DIVING & SNORKELLING

Diving schools organise courses and excursions to the fascinating undersea world. There is a great variety of fish and fascinating underwater fauna. While snorkellers will be able to see small fish close to the shore, divers – with professionals accompanying them – will come face to face with tuna and barracudas further out.
The diving school *Náutico* in San Agustín offers courses ranging from those especially for beginners to trainer certification (1-day course, 75 euros | IFA Interclub Atlantic | Calle Las Jazmines 2 | tel. 9 28 77 81 68). You can book PADI courses and excursions to wrecks, reefs and caves, as well as night dives from *Top Diving* (they also have their own decompression chamber) in Puerto Rico (diving courses from 115 euros | Puerto Escala | tel. 9 28 56 06 09 | www.topdiving.net). The *Club de Mar Hotel* is a popular contact point for diving fans in Puerto de Mogán (tel. 6 89 35 20 49 | www.hotelpuertodemogan.com). And, lovers of the submarine world should get in touch with the *Dive Center* (tel. 9 28 73 61 96 | www.diveacademy-grancanaria. com) in Arguineguín.

## GOLF

There are several 9 and 18-hole courses that invite golf fans to tee off and practise putting all year long. They all have driving ranges, a club house, golf school and shop. The *Real Club de Golf de Las Palmas* is located in a fairy-tale environment high up in the mountains near Santa Brígida. Reservations are necessary (green fee

Hiking between pine forests and reservoirs in the Caldera de la Presa de las Niñas

from 85 euros | tel. 9 28 35 10 50 | www. realgolfclubdelasplamas.com). The Campo de Golf Maspalomas is rather flat; reservations are essential in winter (green fee 95 euros | daily 9am–7pm | Avda. T.O. Neckermann | tel. 9 28 76 25 81 | www. maspalomasgolf.net).

The 18-hole Meloneras Golf course has been laid out attractively between the holiday resort of the same name and Pasito Blanco (green fee 93 euros | daily 8am–7pm | Calle Cánonigo 6 | tel. 9 28 14 53 09 | www. lopesanhr.com). The two 18-hole courses at Salobre Golf (green fee 80–95 euros | daily 10am–6pm | tel. 9 28 01 01 03 | www. salobregolfresort.com) were developed on hilly terrain along the GC 1 to Arguineguín (Salobre Golf exit). The relatively inexpensive 9-hole course INSIDER TIP Anfi Tauro Golf (green fee 36 euros) slopes gently up to the middle of the valley. A round on the 18-hole complex next to it costs close to 100 euros (daily 9am–6pm | Valle de Tauro, at the end of the GC 1 | tel. 9 28 56 04 62 | www.anfitauro.es).

## HIKING

For centuries the caminos reales (paths that were under the direct control of the crown) connected isolated villages with each other. With the introduction of tarmac roads, they fell into oblivion. However, people started to repair them again as tourism developed. In the meantime, many have been surfaced and some of them are also well signposted. You should never just set out on a mountain hike on the spur of the moment as it is very easy to get lost! A good guide book is essential. If you prefer to hike in a group, you can take part on many organised tours that leave from the tourist resorts. For example, Freemotion, in the south of the island, offers tours at all levels of difficulty (Avda. Alféreces Provisionales | Hotel Sandy Beach |

Playa del Inglés | tel. 9 28 77 74 79 | www. free-motion.net | tours from 40 euros). The Grupo Montañero Mogán is a non-commercial group that organises day tours starting in Arguineguín on Sunday mornings (tel., information and registration 647 58 06 33 | www.trekkingmogan.com).

## SAILING

Sailing has a long tradition on the Canary Islands. Hobby sailors can charter yachts in Puerto de Mogán. Sail & Surf Overschmidt in Puerto Rico is the sailing school with the best reputation on Gran Canaria. It organises courses (from 230 euros) for all patents and rents out small boats for 19 euros an hour (Puerto Escala | tel. 9 28 56 52 92).

## WINDSURFING

The northeast trade winds blow regularly along Gran Canaria's coast and, as a result, windsurfing has become the number one sport on many of the island's beaches. Conditions are better in the south in winter (wind force 3–6). Beginners will find things easier in sheltered bays such as Puerto Rico. The real cracks will relish the superb conditions in the north in summer (wind force 5–9). The best location is Pozo Izquierdo (force always 6+). A little further to the south in Playa del Águila, the 33-time world champion Björn Dunckerbeck has run a surf school and provided service facilities for many years (from 45 euros a day, courses for beginners 120 euros | Dunckerbeck Side Shore | Plaza Hibiscus | Playa del Águila | tel. 9 28 76 29 58 | www. sideshore-es.com).

The windsurfing school Mistral operates out of Bahía Feliz (beginners 180 euros | board rental from 65 euros per day | Playa del Tarajalillo | tel. 9 28 15 71 58 | www. club-mistral.com).

# TRAVEL WITH KIDS

**The main holiday complexes have pools and playgrounds specially for children and often provide childcare and organised activities.**

Beaches such as Playa de la Verga, Playa de Puerto Rico and Playa Amadores are protected from the wind and waves and are ideal places for young children to swim safely.

## LAS PALMAS

**INSIDER TIP LOS REYES MAGOS/ CARNIVAL** (131 E2) *(𝄞 H 2)*

Spanish children get their Christmas pre- sents on 6 January (Epiphany), Spanish:

*Reyes Magos*. The Canarios like children above all else and there are even special events for the little ones during carnival. They elect their own Carnival Queen, take part in processions dressed in fantastic costumes and celebrate special fiestas. These are held in Las Palmas and Mas- palomas in Feb. The tourist offices have detailed information on all events. *www. grancanaria.com*

## THE SOUTH

**AQUALAND** (134 A5) *(𝄞 E 7)*

The Aqualand water park in Barranco de Palmitos beyond Maspalomas covers 32

Photo: Caravan of camels in the dunes of Maspalomas

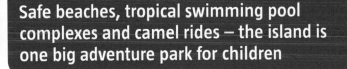

**Safe beaches, tropical swimming pool complexes and camel rides – the island is one big adventure park for children**

acres, has dozens of water slides (all supervised); some are more than 150m long and you ride down on rafts. Please note that children have to be a minimum height to be allowed to use some of the slides! There is 5300m² of pool surface, including a wave pool. You can drift leisurely through the grounds on an artificial river. The children's pools with all kinds of water games and colourful fairy-tale figures will appeal to youngsters. But be careful – there are wide areas of lawn and luxuriant vegetation and it is easy for parents to lose sight of their children – and more difficult to find them again. Cafeterias and bars; extra charge for sunbeds, lockers, etc. The park is suitable for children above 4. *Daily 10am–5pm | entrance 25 euros, children 17.50 euros | approach along the GC 500 and GC 503, follow signs to Parques*

*Temáticos on the right after 3km (1¾mi) | www.aqualand.es/grancanaria*

### AQUAPARK ATLÁNTIDA
(132 C5) (*∭ C 7*)

This water park, beautifully located on a slope in Puerto Rico, has various slides, several swimming pools, water games for children and a cafeteria. Unfortunately, the fun is often disturbed by building projects. All of the slides are supervised and the complex is well suited for children from the age of 4. *Daily 10am–5.30pm | entrance fee 22.50 euros, children 16 euros | 400m beyond the shopping centre | www.villaatlantida.com*

### CAMELS
The *camel station* is on the edge of the dunes (134 B6) (*∭ E 8*) above the Charca

A bronze dog with the patience of Job

de Maspalomas. 30-minute rides across the ocean of sand cost 12 euros, 7 euros for children *(daily 9am–4pm)*. You can also visit the *Camel Safari Park La Baranda* (134 B3) (*∭ E 6*), a little over a mile south of Fataga, with around 100 camels including several young ones *(daily 9am–5pm | 30-minute rides 20 euros, with lunch 31.50 euros, children half-price | tel. 9 28 79 86 80)*.

### HOLIDAY WORLD
(134 B5) (*∭ E 8*)

This leisure centre near Maspalomas has many attractions for kids. The centre of the complex is a fairground with a big wheel, boat swings, merry-go-round, roller coaster, car scooters, pirates' ship and other fun vehicles. Older children will probably be more interested in the electronic games – from pinball machines to virtual car races. You pay separately for each attraction using a chip card bought when you enter. Suitable for children from the age of 6. *Sun–Thu 5.30pm–11pm, Fri/Sat 5.30pm–midnight | Campo Internacional/Avda. Touroperador TUI s/n | www.holidayworld-maspalomas.com*

### LAGO TAURITO
(132 C4) (*∭ C 7*)

The large pool area covers more than 2000m² and is surrounded by tropical vegetation, palm trees, alcoves and open spaces as well as tennis courts, a crazy-golf course and a playground for small children. Bridges span the lakes and there are several slides, small waterfalls and pools for babies too. The bar and restaurant are located on two large islands. An additional charge is made for umbrellas. The complex is well suited to children from the age of 8. *Daily 10am–6pm | entrance fee 11 euros, children 5.50 euros, buffet 10 euros | in the Taurito holiday resort*

**MINI TREN** (134 B5) (*Ⅲ E 7*)

Exploring Playa del Inglés on a small 19th-century-style train is a novel experience. The locomotive pulls four small carriages behind it on its 30 min. sightseeing tour. Descriptions of the main sights in Playa del Inglés are given during the excursion. You will find out all about the dunes of Maspalomas and the lighthouse, chug past luxury hotels and enormous shopping centres: a relaxed pleasure for the whole family. *Daily 11am–noon and 2pm–5pm, every hour | fare: 6 euros, children 3 euros | departure Avda. de Italia*

**PALMITOS PARK** ★ (134 A4) (*Ⅲ E 7*)

In the best leisure park on Gran Canaria, you and your children will not only be able to admire the great variety of Canarian flora but also all the different kinds of animals. Soon after you enter, you will be welcomed by a cage full of charming meerkats; later, you come across gigantic monitor lizards and Australian wallabies. There are dozens of exotic birds – mainly parrots, but also flamingos, pelicans, emus, toucans, owls and hummingbirds – in the huge aviaries, some of which you can go into. The bird-of-prey show *(daily 11.45 am and 2.30pm)* is fascinating, as are the caimans. Lar gibbons and orang-utans live on an island at the bottom of the valley. There is also a butterfly and orchid house, a cactus garden and a large tropical aquarium. Marine mammals perform their tricks in the Delfinarium that was opened in 2010 *(daily 1pm and 4pm)*. Other animal shows *(parrots daily, 10.30am and 11.30am; 2.30pm, 3.30pm and 4.30pm)* make sure that you are entertained. (Expensive) cafeterias and restaurants take care of all your creature comforts. The entire park is extremely well cared-for. And the pleasure of being in this wonderful environment in the middle of a pristine, green valley is thrown in free of charge. *Daily*

A colourful inhabitant of Palmitos Park

*10am–5pm | entrance fee 28.50 euros, children between 4–12, 12 euros | Barranco de Palmitos, around 6 miles north of Maspalomas | bus, single fare 1.60 euros | www.palmitospark.es*

**YUMBO** (134 C5) (*Ⅲ E 8*)

There is a large playground for children in the CC Yumbo shopping centre in Playa del Inglés with trampolines and bungees. *Daily, approx. 6pm 11pm*

**YUPI PARK** (134 C5) (*Ⅲ E 8*)

This leisure park in San Agustín has a separate area with special amusements for children up to the age of 6 *(3 euros)*, as well as video games, trampolines and billiards for those who are a little older *(50 cents – 1 euro per game). Daily 4pm–midnight | upper floor of the San Agustín shopping centre*

# FESTIVALS & EVENTS

There always seems to be a procession taking place somewhere on the island all year round; sometimes for a saint, other times they are music and dance festivals.

## PUBLIC HOLIDAYS

**1 Jan** *Año Nuevo* (New Year's Day); **6 Jan** *Los Reyes* (Epiphany); **19 March** *San José* (St Joseph's Day); **March/April** *Viernes Santo* (Good Friday) – there are magnificent processions in many towns and villages during *Semana Santa* (Holy Week); **1 May** *Día del Trabajo* (Labour Day); **30 May** *Día de las Islas Canarias* (Canary Islands' Day); **May/June** *Corpus Cristi* – solemn processions in Arucas and Las Palmas; **25 July** *Santiago Apóstol* (St James' Day) – fiestas in Gáldar and San Bartolomé de Tirajana; **15 Aug** *Asunción* (Assumption); **8 Sept** *Día de la Virgen del Pino* (Day of the Virgin of the Pine, the patron saint of the island); **12 Oct** *Día de la Hispanidad* (Columbus Day); **1 Nov** *Todos los Santos* (All Saints' Day); **6 Dec** *Día de la Constitución* (Constitution Day); **8 Dec** *Inmaculada Concepción* (Immaculate Conception); **25 Dec** *Navidad* (Christmas Day)

## FESTIVALS & EVENTS

### JANUARY/FEBRUARY
▶ *Festival de Música de Canarias:* International festival (concerts, ballet) in Las Palmas *(www.festivaldecanarias.com)*

### FEBRUARY/MARCH
▶ *Almendros en Flor:* The main 'Almond Blossom Festivals' are in Tejeda and Valsequillo; ▶ *Carnival:* Weeks of dancing, parades and spectacular fireworks *(www.lpacarnaval.com)*

### MARCH
▶ *Festival de Ópera:* World class performances in Las Palmas *(www.operalaspalmas.org);* ▶ *Rally de Canarias:* The island's major rally starts and finishes at Parque Santa Catalina in Las Palmas *(www.rallydecanarias.com)*

### APRIL
▶ *Albaricoques en Flor:* Apricot Blossom Festival in Fataga
▶ *Fiesta de Ansite:* To commemorate the native Canarian battles (Santa Lucía; 29 April)

The absolute highlight is carnival: Canarian fiestas have their roots in religion, folklore or simple joie-de-vivre

## JUNE
▶ *Día de San Juan:* Founding of the city of Las Palmas (24 June)

## JULY
▶ *Nuestra Señora del Carmen:* 16 July, the patron saint of fishermen is remembered in Las Palmas, Gáldar, La Aldea de San Nicolás; boat processions in Arguineguín und Puerto de Mogán

## JULY/AUGUST
▶ *Festival de Teatro y Danza Las Palmas:* Festival with modern dance and contemporary theatre in the capital *(www.teatroydanzalaspalmas.com)*
▶ ⭐ *Bajada de la Rama:* 'Bringing down the branch' on 4 Aug is one of the most picturesque festivals and an old Canarian custom. Pine branches are taken down to the sea where the water is then beaten to plead for rain in the coming months

## SEPTEMBER
▶ INSIDER TIP *Romería Virgen del Pino:* The most important religious pilgrimage on the Canarian archipelago takes place in Teror on 7 and 8 Sept
▶ *Fiesta del Charco:* The 'Pond Festival' in La Aldea de San Nicolás on 10 Sept dates back to 1766 when the bishop discovered people swimming nude in the village pond

## OCTOBER
▶ *Nuestra Señora del Rosario:* Traditional festival in Agüimes on 5 Oct with competitions and *lucha Canaria*
▶ *La Naval:* The Spaniards' victory over the fleet of Sir Francis Drake is celebrated in Las Palmas on 6 Oct

## NOVEMBER
▶ *WOMAD (World of Music and Dance):* 3-day, open-air ethnic music festival in Las Palmas *(www.womad.org)*

# LINKS, BLOGS, APPS & MORE

LINKS

▶ www.panoramio.com The pictures linked with the Google map of the island show even the most remote villages on Gran Canaria (just enter the name of the village)

▶ www.grancanaria.com The Gran Canaria official tourism website: accomodation, climate, sun, beaches, pictures, maps, culture, parties, fun, relax, golf, sport …

▶ www.fotosdegrancanaria.com Almost 20,000 images of the island, sorted by location, can be viewed in this photo gallery

▶ www.worldcruising.com/arc At ARC; the 3000 nautical-mile race from Gran Canaria to the Caribbean (every year, around 20 November) can be followed, almost in real time, via Google Earth

▶ www.gran-canaria-info.com Gran Canaria search engine with tourist information, weather, photos, cheap accommodation, maps, hotels, bars & discos, restaurants, rent-a-cars, gay info, property, etc.

BLOGS & FORUMS

▶ www.gran-canaria-insider.info Forum on the island with up-to-date news and an archive – users must register first

▶ www.gran-canaria-info.com Visitors and *residentes*, foreigners living on Gran Canaria, describe life on the island: with texts, photos and videos

▶ www.rastatun.blogspot.com Site with photos from the less-well-known west of the island with Canarian background music (texts in Spanish)

Regardless of whether you are still preparing your trip or already in Gran Canaria: these addresses will provide you with more information, videos and networks to make your holiday even more enjoyable

VIDEOS & PODCASTS

▶ elviajero.elpais.com/videos/canarias Spain's largest daily newspaper presents a short film on the south of the island in 'El Oasis de Maspalomas' (in Spanish)

▶ www.grancanaria.com/patronato_turismo/17317.0.html The island's tourism authority shows Gran Canaria from its best side: idyllic villages and beautiful scenery

▶ www.youtube.com/watch?v=3usdjPQsOiY Atmospheric and beautifully filmed video of the beach and ocean at Playa de las Canteras in Las Palmas, the extraordinary city beach

▶ radiolingua.com/shows/spanish/coffee-break-spanish Learn Spanish using a course that has consistently been among the top language-learning podcasts in iTunes US and UK and won the European Award for Languages in 2007 and the European Professional Podcast Award in 2009

APPS

▶ Star Walk At night, the starry sky in the mountains on Gran Canaria is absolutely clear. Integrated sensors determine the direction

▶ Suntimer GPS makes it possible to determine your precise position as well as the ultra-violet radiation and compare it with your skin type – the display shows you how long you can stay in the sun

▶ Tunewiki This app for fans of Canarian music gives the lyrics of the songs as well as translations – Musicmap lets you know if anyone nearby is listening to the same songs

▶ FreeTranslator Enter an English text and the audible translation is given

NETWORK

▶ www.dopplr.com You will be informed by mail or text if one of your Facebook friends is on holiday on Gran Canaria at the same time as you

▶ www.facebook.com/pages/Gran-Canaria/36859890434 This Facebook site for Gran Canaria fans provides useful tips, video links and many amusing things

# TRAVEL TIPS

## ARRIVAL

🛬 The cheapest and most convenient way to reach Gran Canaria is by taking a charter flight. A lot of companies offer direct flights to Gran Canaria, with departures often from provincial airports. Flying time: four to five hours. The frequency of flights and prices vary considerably depending on the time of year, so it is worth spending some time comparing. For visitors from outside Europe, the best bet is to fly to Madrid and take an inland flight to Las Palmas.

Gando airport is around 30 to 60 minutes from the main holiday resorts. Buses depart from the arrival level for Las Palmas (every 30 minutes; bus number 60, 2.20 euros) and Playa del Inglés/Maspalomas (once an hour; bus numbers 5 and 6, 3.85 euros). There is an express bus to Puerto Rico and Puerto de Mogán every hour (bus numbers 91 and 1, 6–8 euros); however, they do not depart from the arrival

## RESPONSIBLE TRAVEL

It doesn't take a lot to be environmentally friendly whilst travelling. Don't just think about your carbon footprint whilst flying to and from your holiday destination but also about how you can protect nature and culture abroad. As a tourist it is especially important to respect nature, look out for local products, cycle instead of driving, save water and much more. If you would like to find out more about eco-tourism please visit: *www.ecotourism.org*

hall but from the bust stop on the motorway (300 yards from the airport!). A taxi to Maspalomas costs around 40 euros, to Puerto Rico about 55 euros and 65 euros to Puerto de Mogán.

🚢 A car ferry operated by the *Compañia Trasmediterránea/Acciona* sails from Cádiz every Saturday at around 5pm. The journey to Las Palmas takes about 32 hours; single fare: approximately 280 euros per person, cars around 270 euros. If you intend to do this in winter, make sure you reserve well in advance, if you don't want to be left behind – either on the Internet *(www.trasmediterranea.es)* or through a travel agency.

## BANKS & CREDIT CARDS

You can withdraw money from cash dispensers using your EC card or any of the usual credit cards. However, there are sometimes hefty charges – especially if you use a credit card! Tip: many British banks have local branches or agreements with Spanish banks. You can avoid extra charges if you withdraw your money from them. Check before you leave home. Bank opening hours vary but most are open from 8.30am–2pm, Mon–Fri and from 8.30 am–1pm on Sat. Almost all hotels, and many shops, restaurants and petrol stations accept credit cards. Some useful numbers to block credit cards are: Visa: *tel. 9 00 99 11 24*, Euro and MasterCard: *tel. 9 00 97 12 31*.

## BUSES

The scheduled bus services provided by *Global* leave regularly, and reliably, for the

# From arrival to weather

**Holiday from start to finish: the most important addresses and information for your trip to Gran Canaria**

south of the island from the central bus station *Estación de Guaguas* under *Parque San Telmo* in Las Palmas. The holiday resorts are connected every 15 to 30 minutes between 7am and 11pm. Numbers 30, 50 and 91 are express buses that hardly make any stops on their journey from the south to Las Palmas (timetables are available in the tourist offices and in the ticket office in Parque San Telmo *(Las Palmas | tel. 9 02 38 11 10 | www.globalsu. net)*. The bus services in the north are not as frequent, the connections are sometimes rather complicated and you should count on lengthy waits.

Red hibiscus blooms everywhere on the island

## CAMPING

In principle, pitching your tent wherever you want is forbidden on the island. You can only use the public campsites in the mountains if you have permission from the *OIAC (Oficina de Información y Atención al Ciudadano | Calle Profesor Augustín Millares Carló s/n | 35003 Las Palmas | tel. 9 28 21 92 29 | oiac@grancanaria.com | Mon–Fri 8.30am–2pm, Thu also 5–7pm, Sat 9am–noon)*. It is possible to camp in splendid isolation at the campsite in the mountain village of *Temisas (Ctra. Agüimes – Santa Lucía, km 9 | tel. 9 28 79 81 49)*. Camping Tasartico *(Tasartico | tel. 9 28 89 47 15)* is another site miles from anywhere, albeit close to the sea.

## CAR HIRE

Car rental companies have offices at the airport, in the holiday resorts and in many hotels. You can hire a small car for as little as 20 euros a day (including comprehensive insurance) on a weekly basis. The rates offered by Top Car AutoReisen at the airport and in the south *(www.top-car-hire.com)* are hard to beat. Off-road vehicles, motorbikes *(e.g. from Sunfun in Playa del Inglés | www.sunfun-motorrad.com)* and trikes are much more expensive. You have to be at least 21 years old to hire a car and a deposit is usually required.

## CLIMATE & WHEN TO GO

In winter, the temperature in the south, with its dry climate and few clouds, hardly ever falls below 19°C (66°F) and rarely exceeds 24°C (75°F). In summer, temperatures often rise above 30°C (86°F) and stay at that level for several weeks. Temperatures in the mountains are lower and at altitudes above 500m (1500ft) the biting wind can make the nights there bitterly cold. The sea is always between 18°C (64°F) and 23°C (73°F) degrees making it possible to swim 365 days a year. The most pleasant period to visit Gran Canaria is between November and March.

NB: In Spain, it is compulsory to have a yellow emergency vest in the car!

## CUSTOMS

The Canary Islands have a special tax status. For this reason there are restrictions on goods you can take home with you. The limits are: 200 cigarettes, 50 cigars or 250g of tobacco, 1 litre of spirits, 2 litre of wine and 50g of perfume. Check online before leaving home. For tax and duty on goods brought to the UK from the EU see: *www.hmrc.gov.uk/customs/arriving/arrivingeu.htm*

## DRIVING

The roads on the island are generally good and safe. Traffic is only heavy in Las Palmas and Playa del Inglés. The speed limit in towns is 50km/h (30mph), on main roads 90km/h (55mph) and 100km/h (62mph) or 110 km/h (68mph) on the south motorway. The blood alcohol concentration limit is 0.5mg/alcohol per 100ml/blood.

## ELECTRICITY

200 Volts. Adapters are needed for UK appliances.

## EMBASSIES & CONSULATES

**BRITISH CONSULATE**
*Edificio Cataluña | Calle Luis Morote 6–3° | 35007 Las Palmas de Gran Canaria | tel: 9 02 10 93 56 (alternative: 9 13 34 21 94) | ukinspain.fco.gov.uk/en*

**CONSULAR AGENCY OF THE U.S.**
*Los Martínez de Escober, 3, Oficina, 7 | 35007 Las Palmas | tel: 9 28 27 12 59 | www.embassypages.com/missions/embassy18116*

## EMERGENCY SERVICES

In the case of emergency (police, fire brigade, ambulance, accident), call *tel.* 112. The appropriate authority will then

Sun protection is also very important in the mountains – Roque Nublo in the backround

be contacted. This service is also available in English.

## HEALTH

Some people can have difficulties adjusting to the change in climate. However, the greatest risk comes from the strong solar radiation (even if it is cloudy, and even in winter). You should use mineral water for preparing tea or coffee and brushing your teeth. Holidaymakers with a European Health Insurance Card (EHIC) issued by your social-security office will be treated free of charge in casualty wards and hospitals associated with the Spanish *Seguridad Social*. In other cases, you should make sure that you receive a detailed receipt for any treatment received to be able to claim a refund when you return home. Some useful addresses of hospitals and emergency clinics include:

### LAS PALMAS
*Hospital Universitario de Gran Canaria Dr. Negrín | Barranco de la Ballena | tel. 9 28 45 00 00*

### PLAYA DEL INGLÉS/MASPALOMAS/ SAN AGUSTÍN
*Clínica Roca: San Agustín | Calle Buganvilla 1 | tel. 9 28 76 90 04; G.P.: Dr. Martins | Edificio Mercurio II | tel. 9 28 76 30 07; dentists: Grupo Médico | Avda. Touroperador Neckermann 22–24 | tel. 9 28 77 14 94*

Chemists are usually open from 9am–1pm and 4pm–7pm Mon–Fri and 9am–1pm Sat. The sign *Farmacia de Guardia* lets you know where the nearest 24-hour chemist is.

## IMMIGRATION

A passport or identity card is sufficient for EU citizens to enter Spain and there is no control for passengers arriving from EU countries. Children need their own signed ID with a photograph.

# CURRENCY CONVERTER

| £ | € | € | £ |
|---|---|---|---|
| 1 | 1.20 | 1 | 0.85 |
| 3 | 3.60 | 3 | 2.55 |
| 5 | 6 | 5 | 4.25 |
| 13 | 15.60 | 13 | 11 |
| 40 | 48 | 40 | 34 |
| 75 | 90 | 75 | 64 |
| 120 | 144 | 120 | 100 |
| 250 | 300 | 250 | 210 |
| 500 | 600 | 500 | 425 |

| $ | € | € | $ |
|---|---|---|---|
| 1 | 0.75 | 1 | 1.30 |
| 3 | 2.30 | 3 | 3.90 |
| 5 | 3.80 | 5 | 6.50 |
| 13 | 10 | 13 | 17 |
| 40 | 30 | 40 | 50 |
| 75 | 55 | 75 | 97 |
| 120 | 90 | 120 | 155 |
| 250 | 185 | 250 | 325 |
| 500 | 370 | 500 | 650 |

For current exchange rates see www.xe.com

## INFORMATION

### SPANISH TOURIST OFFICE
*Internet: www.spain.info*

### PATRONATO DEL TURISMO
*Mon–Fri 8am–3pm | Calle Léon y Castillo 17 | Las Palmas | tel. 9 28 21 96 00 | www.grancanria.com*

### AIRPORT INFORMATION
*In the arrivals' hall tel. 9 28 57 41 17 | flight information tel. 9 02 40 47 04*

# BUDGETING

| | |
|---|---|
| Taxi | 80p/$1.30 |
| | *for each km travelled* |
| Coffee | min. 80p/$1.30 |
| | *for a café au lait* |
| Snack | min. £2.50/$4 |
| | *per tapa* |
| Letters/cards | 60p/$1.10 |
| | *to friends at home* |
| Petrol | less than 50p/$1.30 |
| | *for 1 litre of* |
| | *Eurosuper* |
| Rides | £10/$16 |
| | *for a camel ride in* |
| | *Maspalomas* |

## INTERNET CAFÉS & WIFI

Many hotels provide WiFi services even if only in specific areas such as the lobby or café. This is not always included in the price of the room; the same applies to computers available for holidaymakers to surf the internet. Public internet cafés, which can often be found in amusement arcades *(salón recreativo)*, are less expensive and usually equipped with a camera and microphone for online telephoning.

## MEDIA

Hotels and holiday complexes have cable and satellite installations so that guests can watch international television programmes. The English radio station Power FM, located in Los Gigantes also broadcasts to the Canary Islands (Gran Canaria: South East: 91.7FM, South West: 91.9FM). It plays music from the '70s–contemporary and includes news, discussions, weather, sport and travel information. Power FM is the largest radio network in the Canary Islands.

## NUDE BATHING

Nude bathing is only common in the central section of the beach between *Playa del Inglés* and *Playa de Maspalomas*. The Oböna travel company runs a naturist hotel in Maspalomas *(www.oboena.de)*.

## OPENING HOURS

On weekdays, shops usually open between 9am and 10am and close at around 8pm. Many smaller shops close for a siesta (1.30pm–5pm). As a rule, work stops at 2pm on Saturday. Large supermarkets and shopping centres are open non-stop from 9am–9pm, Mon–Sat. Most of the 24-hour shops are located near the port in Las Palmas. In the main resort areas in the south, many shops and supermarkets are open from 8am to 10pm, 7 days a week.

## PHONE & MOBILE PHONES

You can call home from any phone box with the *internacional* sign. They also accept the practical telephone cards *(teletarjeta)* that can be bought from newspaper stands for 6 or 12 euros. It is even cheaper to call from the private telephone offices *locutorios*; most of them are in the port area of Las Palmas and calling abroad costs from 10–15 cents a minute. If you activate the EU tariff, you will save roaming charges. It guarantees comparatively low rates but you will still be charged for incoming calls. This can be avoided by using a Spanish prepaid card. Prepaid cards are more expensive but also save on roaming fees and you can get your new number before you leave home. Text messages are always an economical alternative. Mailbox charges are very high. Turn it off before you reach the Canaries! The dialling code is the same as the Spanish mainland 0034.

## PRICES

The prices for services are not much lower than in many other European countries. Themes parks are expensive; the admission for a family of four can easily exceed 100 euros. Tobacco products, perfume and some non-prescription medicines are quite cheap. Groceries, especially local produce, are considerably cheaper than in many cities in Europe.

## SMOKING

In Spain there is a law forbidding smoking in closed spaces; this includes cafés, bars and restaurants. Hotels have special rooms for smokers.

## TAXIS

Taxis are white with a sign with a green light on the roof. They are all licensed and have taximeters. If you want to make a tour in one, agree on the price in advance.

## TIME

The Canaries have GMT all year round.

## TIPPING

If you are satisfied with the service in a restaurant, round up the amount. The cleaning staff in the hotels also expect a tip, as well as bus drivers and guides on organised excursions.

# WEATHER IN LAS PALMAS

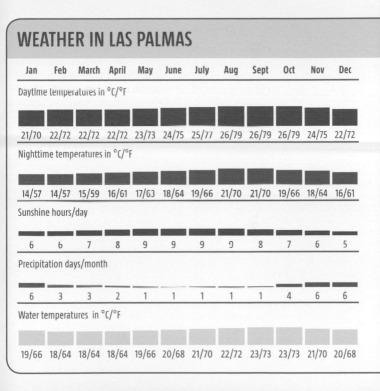

| | Jan | Feb | March | April | May | June | July | Aug | Sept | Oct | Nov | Dec |
|---|---|---|---|---|---|---|---|---|---|---|---|---|
| Daytime temperatures in °C/°F | 21/70 | 22/72 | 22/72 | 22/72 | 23/73 | 24/75 | 25/77 | 26/79 | 26/79 | 26/79 | 24/75 | 22/72 |
| Nighttime temperatures in °C/°F | 14/57 | 14/57 | 15/59 | 16/61 | 17/63 | 18/64 | 19/66 | 21/70 | 21/70 | 19/66 | 18/64 | 16/61 |
| Sunshine hours/day | 6 | 6 | 7 | 8 | 9 | 9 | 9 | 9 | 8 | 7 | 6 | 5 |
| Precipitation days/month | 6 | 3 | 3 | 2 | 1 | 1 | 1 | 1 | 1 | 4 | 6 | 6 |
| Water temperatures in °C/°F | 19/66 | 18/64 | 18/64 | 18/64 | 19/66 | 20/68 | 21/70 | 22/72 | 23/73 | 23/73 | 21/70 | 20/68 |

# USEFUL PHRASES SPANISH

## PRONUNCIATION

| | |
|---|---|
| c | before 'e' and 'i' like 'th' in 'thin' |
| ch | as in English |
| g | before 'e' and 'i' like the 'ch' in Scottish 'loch' |
| gue, gui | like 'get', 'give' |
| que, qui | the 'u' is not spoken, i.e. 'ke', 'ki' |
| j | always like the 'ch' in Scottish 'loch' |
| ll | like 'lli' in 'million'; some speak it like 'y' in 'yet' |
| ñ | 'nj' |
| z | like 'th' in 'thin' |

### IN BRIEF

| | |
|---|---|
| Yes/No/Maybe | sí/no/quizás |
| Please/Thank you | por favor/gracias |
| Hello!/Goodbye!/See you | ¡Hola!/¡Adiós!/¡Hasta luego! |
| Good morning!/afternoon!/ evening!/night! | ¡Buenos días!/¡Buenos días!/¡Buenas tardes!/¡Buenas noches! |
| Excuse me, please! | ¡Perdona!/¡Perdone! |
| May I ...?/Pardon? | ¿Puedo ...?/¿Cómo dice? |
| My name is ... | Me llamo ... |
| What's your name? | ¿Cómo se llama usted?/¿Cómo te llamas? |
| I'm from ... | Soy de ... |
| I would like to .../Have you got ...? | Querría .../¿Tiene usted ...? |
| How much is ...? | ¿Cuánto cuesta ...? |
| I (don't) like that | Esto (no) me gusta. |
| good/bad/broken/doesn't work | bien/mal/roto/no funciona |
| too much/much/little/all/nothing | demasiado/mucho/poco/todo/nada |
| Help!/Attention!/Caution! | ¡Socorro!/¡Atención!/¡Cuidado! |
| ambulance/police/fire brigade | ambulancia/policía/bomberos |
| May I take a photo here | ¿Podría fotografiar aquí? |

### DATE & TIME

| | |
|---|---|
| Monday/Tuesday/Wednesday | lunes/martes/miércoles |
| Thursday/Friday/Saturday | jueves/viernes/sábado |
| Sunday/working day/holiday | domingo/laborable/festivo |
| today/tomorrow/yesterday | hoy/mañana/ayer |

# ¿Hablas español?

**"Do you speak Spanish?"** This guide will help you to say the basic words and phrases in Spanish.

| | |
|---|---|
| hour/minute/second/moment | hora/minuto/segundo/momento |
| day/night/week/month/year | día/noche/semana/mes/año |
| now/immediately/before/after | ahora/enseguida/antes/después |
| What time is it? | ¿Qué hora es? |
| It's three o'clock/It's half past three | Son las tres/Son las tres y media |
| a quarter to four/a quarter past four | cuatro menos cuarto/ cuatro y cuarto |

## TRAVEL

| | |
|---|---|
| open/closed/opening times | abierto/cerrado/horario |
| entrance / exit | entrada/acceso salida |
| departure/arrival | salida/llegada |
| toilets/ladies/gentlemen | aseos/señoras/caballeros |
| free/occupied | libre/ocupado |
| (not) drinking water | agua (no) potable |
| Where is ...?/Where are ...? | ¿Dónde está ...? /¿Dónde están ...? |
| left/right | izquierda/derecha |
| straight ahead/back | recto/atrás |
| close/far | cerca/lejos |
| traffic lights/corner/crossing | semáforo/esquina/cruce |
| bus/tram/U-underground/ | autobús/tranvía/metro/ |
| taxi/cab | taxi |
| bus stop/cab stand | parada/parada de taxis |
| parking lot/parking garage | parking/garaje |
| street map/map | plano de la ciudad/mapa |
| train station/harbour/airport | estación/puerto/aeropuerto |
| ferry/quay | transbordador/muelle |
| schedule/ticket/supplement | horario/billete/suplemento |
| single/return | sencillo/ida y vuelta |
| train/track/platform | tren/vía/andén |
| delay/strike | retraso/huelga |
| I would like to rent ... | Querría ... alquilar |
| a car/a bicycle/a boat | un coche/una bicicleta/un barco |
| petrol/gas station | gasolinera |
| petrol/gas / diesel | gasolina/diesel |
| breakdown/repair shop | avería/taller |

## FOOD & DRINK

| | |
|---|---|
| Could you please book a table for tonight for four? | Resérvenos, por favor, una mesa para cuatro personas para hoy por la noche. |
| on the terrace/by the window | en la terraza/junto a la ventana |

| | |
|---|---|
| The menu, please/ | ¡El menú, por favor! |
| Could I please have ...? | ¿Podría traerme ... por favor? |
| bottle/carafe/glass | botella/jarra/vaso |
| knife/fork/spoon | cuchillo/tenedor/cuchara |
| salt/pepper/sugar | sal/pimienta/azúcar |
| vinegar/oil/milk/cream/lemon | vinagre/aceite/leche/limón |
| cold/too salty/not cooked | frío/demasiado salado/sin hacer |
| with/without ice/sparkling | con/sin hielo/gas |
| vegetarian/allergy | vegetariano/vegetariana/alergía |
| May I have the bill, please? | Querría pagar, por favor. |
| bill/receipt/tip | cuenta/recibo/propina |

## SHOPPING

| | |
|---|---|
| pharmacy/chemist | farmacia/droguería |
| baker/market | panadería/mercado |
| butcher/fishmonger | carnicería/pescadería |
| shopping centre/department store | centro comercial/grandes almacenes |
| shop/supermarket/kiosk | tienda/supermercado/quiosco |
| 100 grammes/1 kilo | cien gramos/un kilo |
| expensive/cheap/price/more/less | caro/barato/precio/más/menos |
| organically grown | de cultivo ecológico |

## ACCOMMODATION

| | |
|---|---|
| I have booked a room | He reservado una habitación. |
| Do you have any ... left? | ¿Tiene todavía ...? |
| single room/double room | habitación individual/habitación doble |
| breakfast/half board/ | desayuno/media pensión/ |
| full board (American plan) | pensión completa |
| at the front/seafront/garden view | hacia delante/hacia el mar/hacia el jardín |
| shower/sit-down bath | ducha/baño |
| balcony/terrace | balcón/terraza |
| key/room card | llave/tarjeta |
| luggage/suitcase/bag | equipaje/maleta/bolso |
| swimming pool/spa/sauna | piscina/spa/sauna |
| soap/toilet paper/nappy (diaper) | jabón/papel higiénico/pañal |
| cot/high chair/nappy changing | cuna/trona/cambiar los pañales |
| deposit | anticipo/caución |

## BANKS, MONEY & CREDIT CARDS

| | |
|---|---|
| bank/ATM/ | banco/cajero automático/ |
| pin code | número secreto |
| cash/credit card | en efectivo/tarjeta de crédito |
| bill/coin/change | billete/moneda/cambio |

## HEALTH

| | |
|---|---|
| doctor/dentist/paediatrician | médico/dentista/pediatra |
| hospital/emergency clinic | hospital/urgencias |
| fever/pain/inflamed/injured | fiebre/dolor/inflamado/herido |
| diarrhoea/nausea/sunburn | diarrea/náusea/quemadura de sol |
| plaster/bandage/ointment/cream | tirita/vendaje/pomada/crema |
| pain reliever/tablet/suppository | calmante/comprimido/supositorio |

## POST, TELECOMMUNICATIONS & MEDIA

| | |
|---|---|
| stamp/letter/postcard | sello/carta/postal |
| I need a landline phone card/ | Necesito una tarjeta telefónica/ |
| I'm looking for a prepaid card for my mobile | Busco una tarjeta prepago para mi móvil |
| Where can I find internet access? | ¿Dónde encuentro un acceso a internet? |
| dial/connection/engaged | marcar/conexión/ocupado |
| socket/adapter/charger | enchufe/adaptador/cargador |
| computer/battery/ rechargeable battery | ordenador/batería/ batería recargable |
| e-mail address/at sign (@) | (dirección de) correo electrónico/arroba |
| internet address (URL) | dirección de internet |
| internet connection/wifi | conexión a internet/wifi |
| e-mail/file/print | archivo/imprimir |

## LEISURE, SPORTS & BEACH

| | |
|---|---|
| beach/sunshade/lounger | playa/sombrilla/tumbona |
| low tide/high tide/current | marea baja/marea alta/corriente |

## NUMBERS

| | | | |
|---|---|---|---|
| 0 | cero | 14 | catorce |
| 1 | un, uno, una | 15 | quince |
| 2 | dos | 16 | dieciséis |
| 3 | tres | 17 | diecisiete |
| 4 | cuatro | 18 | dieciocho |
| 5 | cinco | 19 | diecinueve |
| 6 | seis | 20 | veinte |
| 7 | siete | 100 | cien, ciento |
| 8 | ocho | 200 | doscientos, doscientas |
| 9 | nueve | 1000 | mil |
| 10 | diez | 2000 | dos mil |
| 11 | once | 10 000 | diez mil |
| 12 | doce | 1/2 | medio |
| 13 | trece | 1/4 | un cuarto |

# NOTES

# FOR YOUR NEXT HOLIDAY ...

# MARCO POLO TRAVEL GUIDES

ALGARVE
AMSTERDAM
AUSTRALIA
BANGKOK
BARCELONA
BERLIN
BRUSSELS
BUDAPEST
CALIFORNIA
CAPE TOWN
  WINE LANDS,
  GARDEN ROUTE
COLOGNE
CORFU
GRAN CANARIA
CRETE
CUBA
CYPRUS
  NORTH AND
  SOUTH
DUBAI

DUBROVNIK &
  DALMATIAN COAST
EDINBURGH
EGYPT
FINLAND
FLORIDA
FRENCH RIVIERA
  NICE, CANNES &
  MONACO
HONGKONG
  MACAU
IRELAND
ISRAEL
ISTANBUL
JORDAN
KOS
LAKE GARDA

LANZAROTE
LAS VEGAS
LONDON
LOS ANGELES
MADEIRA
  PORTO SANTO
MALLORCA
MALTA
  GOZO
MOROCCO
NEW YORK
NEW ZEALAND
NORWAY
PARIS
RHODES

ROME
SAN FRANCISCO
SICILY
SOUTH AFRICA
STOCKHOLM
TENERIFE
THAILAND
TURKEY
  SOUTH COAST
UNITED ARAB
  EMIRATES
VENICE
VIETNAM

- PACKED WITH INSIDER TIPS
- BEST WALKS AND TOURS
- FULL-COLOUR PULL-OUT MAP
  AND STREET ATLAS

# ROAD ATLAS

The green line ▬▬▬ indicates the Trips & Tours (p. 96–101)
The blue line ▬▬ indicates the perfect route (p. 30–31)

All tours are also marked on the pull-out map

Photo: Las Palmas, Playa de las Canteras

# Exploring Gran Canaria

The map on the back cover shows how the area has been sub-divided

A     B     C

**1**

2km
1.24 mi

Santa Cruz de Tenerife

P
Punta de Sard

**2**

O C É A N O    A T L Á N T I C O

Roqu

Punta

Punta del Caro

Punta del Tur

★ Puerto
de las Niev

★ Dedo a
Playa de Gua

**3**

Playa de Sotave
Punta de la Palma

Playa Segura

La Laja del Risco

Cruz del
Tabaibal

102

El Risco

Punta Góngora

Playa del Risco

Los Lla

**4**

6

39 Parq

Andén Verde

11

Casas de Tirma

La Fajana

GC200

12

Mirador de Balcón

2013

Punta de la
Aldea

Carrizo

493

Casas de Lentisco

de Tanadaba

1015

Caserones

Puerto de la Aldea
Playa de la Aldea

819

**5**   P. de los Agujeros

Las
Marciegas

Albercón

4

La Aldea
de San Nicolás

Embalse de
San Nicolás

Roque Colorado

790

Los Espinos

(64)

2.5

G

7.5

Amurga

1.5

Barranco de la Aldea

Los Molinos

Embalse
Caidero de la Niña

Emba

**6**   P. de la Soga

Punta del Peñón

Bermejo

P. de Güigüí Chico

Playa de Güigüí

Artejévez

2.5

Montaña

de

la F

c as
de Pino Gordo

Viso

997

Tocodomán

Mña
de Horgazales

1042

132

128

21

GC200

Degollada de la Aldea

5

1426

Mña de
las Monjas

1471

Casillas

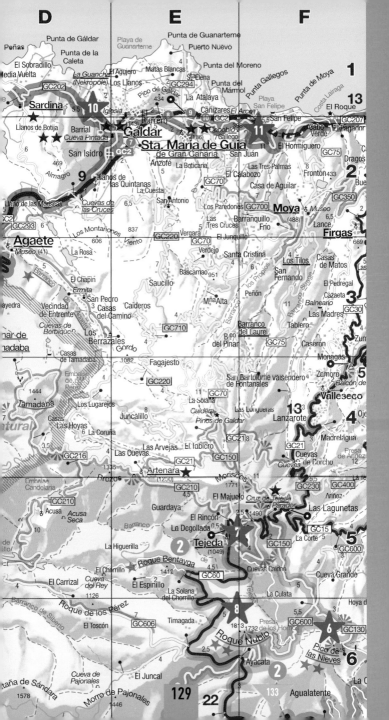

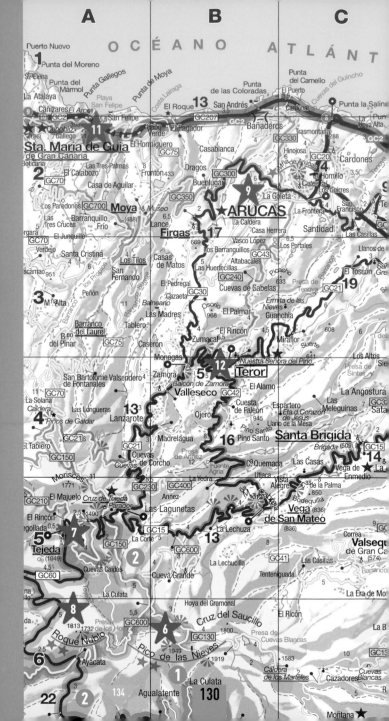

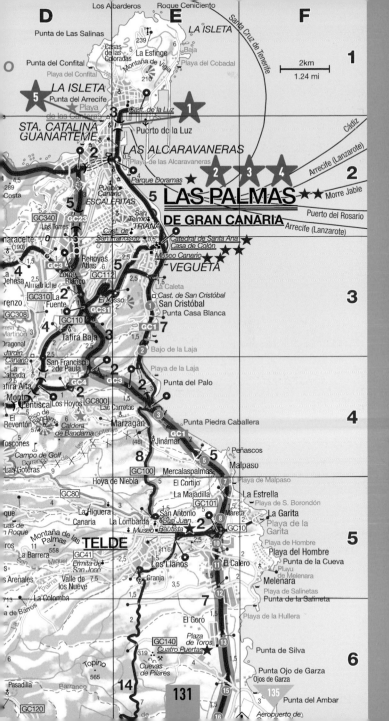

**D**    **E**    **F**

Los Albarderos   Roque Ceniciento

Santa Cruz de Tenerife

**LA ISLETA**

Punta de Las Salinas

Casas de las Coloradas   239

La Esfinge

Punta del Confital   Montaña de Vigia   Playa del Cobadal

Baja

Playa del Confital   210

**1**

2km
1.24 mi

**LA ISLETA**

⭐ **5**   Punta del Arrecife

Cast. de la Luz   ⭐ **1**

Playa de las Canteras

Cádiz

**STA. CATALINA**   Puerto de la Luz

**GUANARTEME**

**LAS ALCARAVANERAS**

Arrecife (Lanzarote)

**2**

Playa de las Alcaravaneras

⭐ **2**   ⭐ **3**   ⭐ **4**

Parque Doramas ⭐

Morre Jable

Pueblo Canario

**LAS PALMAS**

⭐⭐

**ESCALERITAS**

**5**

San Telmo

**DE GRAN CANARIA**

Puerto del Rosario

GC340   GC23

Las Torres

Cast. de

**TRIANA**

Arrecife (Lanzarote)

San Francisco

Catedral de Santa Ana ⭐

Casa de Colón ⭐

Rehoyas   GC3   Atlas

Museo Canario ⭐⭐

GC112

**VEGUETA**

La Caleta

**4**   Dehesa

Almatriche   Lomo Blanco

GC310   La Fuente

El Lasso

Cast. de San Cristóbal

**3**

renzo   GC308

GC31

San Cristóbal

GC110

Punta Casa Blanca

Tafira Baja

GC1

San Francisco de Paula

Bajo de la Laja

GC4   GC3

Playa de la Laja

Tafira Alta

Los Hoyos   GC800

Punta del Palo

Monte   Lentiscal

Las Carretoc

El Reventón   Caldera de Bandama

Marzagán

Punta Piedra Caballera

**4**

Campo de Golf

GC1

Jinámar

Peñascos

Toscones

Malpaso

**8**

Las Goteras

GC100   Mercalaspalmas

**5**   **5**

Playa de Malpaso

Hoya de Niebla

El Cortijo

**7**

La Estrella

GC80

La Majadilla

GC101

Playa de S. Borondón

La Higuera   Canaria

La Lombarda

San Antonio

Mareta

**La Garita**

Museo   San Juan Bautista

**8**

GC10

Playa de la Garita

**TELDE**

**2**

La Barrera   GC41

Montaña de las Palmas

**10**

Playa de Hombre

Ermita de San José

558

Miguel

Los Llanos

**11**

El Calero

**Playa del Hombre**

s Arenales

Valle de los Nueve

Granja

Punta de la Cueva

La Colomba

**12**

**Melenara**

a de Barros

**7**

Playa de Salinetas

El Goro

Punta de la Salineta

Playa de la Hullera

GC140

Plaza de Toros

**13**

Topino

Cuatro Puertas ⭐

Punta de Silva

565

Cuevas de Pilares

Punta Ojo de Garza

**6**

Pasadilla   Barranco

**14**

**131**   **15**   **135**   Punta del Ambar

GC120

**16**   Aeropuerto de

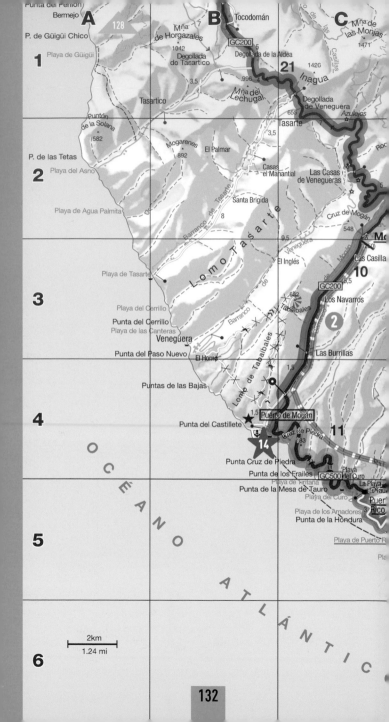

Punta del Peñón
Bermejo
Tocodomán
Mña de las Monjas

P. de Güigüi Chico
**A** 128
Mña de Horgazales
1042
**B**
GC200
Mña de las Casillas
1471
**C**

**1**
Playa de Güigüi
Degollada do Tasartico
Degollada de la Aldea
21
1426

3.5
996
Inagua

Tasartico
Mña del Lechugal
Degollada de Veneguera
655
Azulejos

Puntón de la Solana
582
Tasarte
3.5

P. de las Tetas
Playa del Asno
Mogarenes
892
El Palmar
Casas el Manantial
Las Casas de Venegueras

**2**
Playa de Agua Palmita
Santa Brigida
8
Cruz de Mogán
548

Playa de Tasarte
Lomo Tasarte
El Inglés
Veneguera
9.5
Mo

Playa del Cerrillo
Barranco de Tasarte
GC200
Las Casillas
**10**
5.5

Punta del Cerrillo
Playa de las Canteras
Veneguera
Barranco
Tabaibales
642
Los Navarros
**2**

**3**
Punta del Paso Nuevo
El Horno
Las Burrillas

Puntas de las Bajas
Lomo de Tabaibales
1.5

**4**
Punta del Castillete
Puerto de Mogán
1.5
**11**

**14**
Cruz de Piedra
1.33

Punta Cruz de Piedra
Punta de los Frailes
GC500
Playa del Curo
La Playa de Tau

Punta de la Mesa de Tauro
Playa de Tiritana
Playa del Curo
Puer Rico

Playa de los Amadores
Punta de la Hondura
3

**5**
Playa de Puerto R
Pla

O C É A N O   A T L Á N T I C O

2km
1.24 mi

**6**
132

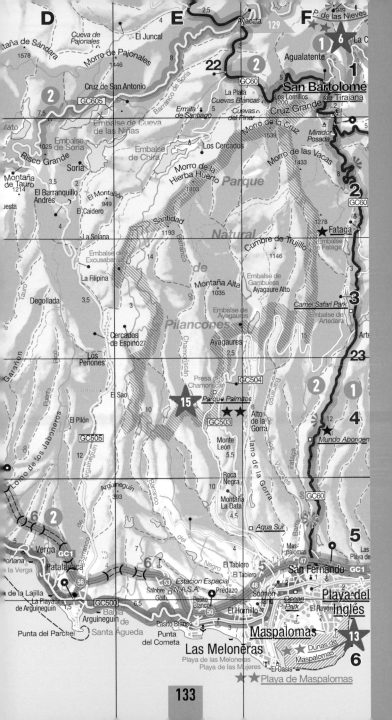

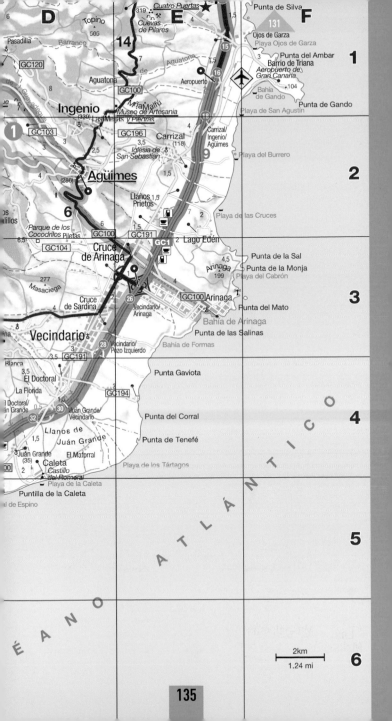

**D**

Pasadilla

Topino
505

Barranco

GC120

Aguatona

Ingenio

GC103

GC100

**1**

8

Museo de Artesania

Las Mejías y Piedras
(339)

GC196

Iglesia de
San Sebastián

Agüimes
(286)

**6**

3,5

2,5

1,5

Parque de los
Cocodrilos Piletas

GC100

GC104

Cruce
de Arinaga

GC191

GC1

277

Masaciega

Cruce
de Sardina

Vecindario/
Arinaga

26

Vecindario

28

Vecindario/
Pozo Izquierdo

GC191

3,5

El Doctoral

GC194

La Florida

El Doctoral/
án Grande

32

30

0,5

1,0

Juan Grande/
Vecindario

Llanos de
Juán Grande

1,5

Juán Grande
(35)

Caleta
Castillo
del Romeral

El Matorral

Playa de la Caleta

Puntilla de la Caleta

al de Espino

**E**

319

Cuatro Puertas ★

Cuevas
de Pilares

**14**

7

de

Mña Malfú

Carrizal
(118)

**9**

Llános
Prietos

Lago Edén

Arinaga
199

GC100

Arinaga

Punta Gaviota

Punta del Corral

Punta de Tenefé

Playa de los Tártagos

**F**

Punta de Silva

131

Ojos de Garza
Playa Ojos de Garza

Punta del Ambar
Barrio de Triana
Aeropuerto de
Gran Canaria

15

Aguatona

Aeropuerto

16

Bahía
de Gando

Punta de Gando

104

Playa de San Agustín

18

Carrizal/
Ingenio/
Agüimes

Playa del Burrero

Playa de las Cruces

Punta de la Sal
Punta de la Monja
Playa del Cabrón

Punta del Mato

Bahía de Arinaga

Punta de las Salinas

Bahía de Formas

**1**

**2**

**3**

**4**

**5**

**6**

O C É A N O   A T L Á N T I C O

2km
1.24 mi

# KEY TO ROAD ATLAS

|  | |  |
|---|---|---|
| Motorway · Toll junction · Toll station · Junction with number · Motel · Restaurant · Snackbar · Filling-station · Parking place with and without WC | Trento · 11 | Autobahn · Gebührenpflichtige Anschlussstelle · Gebührenstelle · Anschlussstelle mit Nummer · Rasthaus mit Übernachtung · Raststätte · Kleinraststätte · Tankstelle · Parkplatz mit und ohne WC |
| Motorway under construction and projected with completion date | Datum   Date | Autobahn in Bau und geplant mit Datum der Verkehrsübergabe |
| Dual carriageway (4 lanes) | | Zweibahnige Straße (4-spurig) |
| Trunk road | | Fernverkehrsstraße |
| Road numbers | 14   E45 | Straßennummern |
| Important main road | | Wichtige Hauptstraße |
| Main road · Tunnel · Bridge | )=( | Hauptstraße · Tunnel · Brücke |
| Minor roads | | Nebenstraßen |
| Track · Footpath | | Fahrweg · Fußweg |
| Tourist footpath (selection) | | Wanderweg (Auswahl) |
| Main line railway | | Eisenbahn mit Fernverkehr |
| Rack-railway, funicular | | Zahnradbahn, Standseilbahn |
| Aerial cableway · Chair-lift | | Kabinenschwebebahn · Sessellift |
| Car ferry · Passenger ferry | | Autofähre · Personenfähre |
| Shipping line | | Schifffahrtslinie |
| Nature reserve · Prohibited area | | Naturschutzgebiet · Sperrgebiet |
| National park, natural park · Forest | | Nationalpark, Naturpark · Wald |
| Road closed to motor vehicles | X X X X X | Straße für Kfz. gesperrt |
| Toll road | | Straße mit Gebühr |
| Road closed in winter | XII-II | Straße mit Wintersperre |
| Road closed or not recommended for caravans | | Straße für Wohnanhänger gesperrt bzw. nicht empfehlenswert |
| Tourist route · Pass | Weinstraße   1510 | Touristenstraße · Pass |
| Scenic view · Panoramic view · Route with beautiful scenery | | Schöner Ausblick · Rundblick · Landschaftlich bes. schöne Strecke |
| Spa · Swimming pool | | Heilbad · Schwimmbad |
| Youth hostel · Camping site | | Jugendherberge · Campingplatz |
| Golf-course · Ski jump | | Golfplatz · Sprungschanze |
| Church · Chapel | | Kirche im Ort, freistehend · Kapelle |
| Monastery · Monastery ruin | | Kloster · Klosterruine |
| Synagogue · Mosque | | Synagoge · Moschee |
| Palace, castle · Ruin | | Schloss, Burg · Schloss-, Burgruine |
| Tower · Radio-, TV-tower | | Turm · Funk-, Fernsehturm |
| Lighthouse · Power station | | Leuchtturm · Kraftwerk |
| Waterfall · Lock | | Wasserfall · Schleuse |
| Important building · Market place, area | | Bauwerk · Marktplatz, Areal |
| Arch. excavation, ruins · Mine | | Ausgrabungs- u. Ruinenstätte · Bergwer |
| Dolmen · Menhir · Nuraghe | π | Dolmen · Menhir · Nuraghen |
| Cairn · Military cemetery | | Hünen-, Hügelgrab · Soldatenfriedhof |
| Hotel, inn, refuge · Cave | | Hotel, Gasthaus, Berghütte · Höhle |

## Culture / Kultur

|  | |  |
|---|---|---|
| Picturesque town · Elevation | WIEN (171) | Malerisches Ortsbild · Ortshöhe |
| Worth a journey | ★★ MILANO | Eine Reise wert |
| Worth a detour | ★ TEMPLIN | Lohnt einen Umweg |
| Worth seeing | Andermatt | Sehenswert |

## Landscape / Landschaft

|  | |  |
|---|---|---|
| Worth a journey | ★★ Las Cañadas | Eine Reise wert |
| Worth a detour | ★ Texel | Lohnt einen Umweg |
| Worth seeing | Dikti | Sehenswert |

## Trips & Tours / Ausflüge & Touren

|  | |  |
|---|---|---|
| **Perfect route** | | **Perfekte Route** |
| **MARCO POLO Highlight** | ★1 | **MARCO POLO Highlight** |

# INDEX

This index lists all places, sights and beaches *(playas)* in this guide.
Numbers in bold indicate a main entry, italics to photographs.

# WRITE TO US

e-mail: info@marcopologuides.co.uk

Did you have a great holiday?
Is there something on your mind?
Whatever it is, let us know!
Whether you want to praise, alert us
to errors or give us a personal tip –
MARCO POLO would be pleased to
hear from you.
We do everything we can to provide the
very latest information for your trip.

Nevertheless, despite all of our authors'
thorough research, errors can creep in.
MARCO POLO does not accept any
liability for this. Please contact us by
e-mail or post.

MARCO POLO Travel Publishing Ltd
Pinewood, Chineham Business Park
Crockford Lane, Chineham
Basingstoke, Hampshire RG24 8AL
United Kingdom

## PICTURE CREDITS

Cover photograph: Playa del Inglés, Maspalomas (Laif: Modrow)
Free Motion Bikes & Tours (16 top); R. Freyer (front flap left, 2 centre top, 2 centre bottom, 3 bottom, 6, 8, 9, 12/13, 21, 24/25, 28, 28/29, 32/33, 34, 36, 38, 40, 42, 60, 62, 72, 80/81, 84/85, 92/93, 94, 96/97, 113); I. Gawin (1 bottom, 2 top, 4, 5, 91, 112 bottom); Gloria Palace Thalasso & Hotels: Celestino Gonzalez (16 bottom); © iStockphoto.com: Paul Gardner (17 bottom), Anthony Mayatt (16 centre); C. Lachenmaier (3 top, 49, 51, 58/59, 71, 78, 82, 112 top, 115); Laif: Modrow (1 top); mauritius images: Alamy (18/19, 26 right, 30 top, 30 bottom, 99, 102/103, 104, 116, 126/127), Ava (7, 100), Otto (52), Schmied (57); Daniel Pérez (17 top); D. Renckhoff (front flap right, 15, 83); White Star: Gumm (2 bottom, 3 centre, 29, 44/45, 46, 74/75, 86, 90, 106/107, 111), Pasdzior (109); T. P. Widmann (10/11, 22, 26 left, 27, 37, 55, 64/65, 67, 69, 76, 87, 89, 108, 110, 110/111, 137), E. Wrba (95)

## 1st Edition 2013

Worldwide Distribution: Marco Polo Travel Publishing Ltd, Pinewood, Chineham Business Park, Crockford Lane, Basingstoke, Hampshire RG24 8AL, United Kingdom. Email: sales@marcopolouk.com
© MAIRDUMONT GmbH & Co. KG, Ostfildern
Chief editors: Michaela Lienemann (concept, managing editor), Marion Zorn (concept, text editor)
Author: Sven Weniger; co-author: Izabella Gawin; editor: Karin Liebe
Programme supervision: Ann-Katrin Kutzner, Nikolai Michaelis, Silwen Randebrock
Picture editor: Gabriele Forst
What's hot: wunder media, Munich
Cartography road atlas & pull-out map: © MAIRDUMONT, Ostfildern
Design: milchhof: atelier, Berlin; Front cover, pull-out map cover, page 1: factor product munich
Translated from German by Robert Scott McInnes; editor of the English edition: Christopher Wynne
Prepress: M. Feuerstein, Wigel
Phrase book in cooperation with Ernst Klett Sprachen GmbH, Stuttgart, Editorial by Pons Wörterbücher
All rights reserved. No part of this book may be reproduced, stored in a retrieval system or transmitted in any form or by any means (electronic, mechanical, photocopying, recording or otherwise) without prior written permission from the publisher.
Printed in Germany on non-chlorine bleached paper

# DOS & DON'TS ✋

Even on Gran Canaria there are some things you should avoid

## DON'T HAVE UNPROTECTED SEX

Surveys of tourists under the age of 26 report that 50% have sex with a new partner while on holiday in the Canaries. This greatly increases the risk of contracting HIV and other diseases. Have fun but be responsible; protect yourself and others!

## DON'T BE TAKEN IN BY SPECIAL OFFERS

Aggressive canvassers try to sell tourists dubious holiday packages. They used to be known as time-sharing but now they have changed their name to 'holiday pack', 'holiday club' etc. These supposedly luxurious holidays turn out to be exorbitantly priced offers and often thousands of euros are demanded up front. Be warned!

## DO BUY ORIGINAL BRANDS

You should only buy watches, electronic goods and top-brand fashions in department stores and shops. The 'bargains' you will be offered in bazaars and flea-markets are always fakes. And, if you buy them, they might end up costing you much more than you thought. British customs can confiscate these goods and impose a hefty fine.

## DO KEEP YOUR EYES OPEN

Hired cares are broken into and valuables stolen at the beach or in the hotels in Las Palmas and the tourist resorts. Don't leave anything in your car or any items of value lying around in your hotel room or holiday flat! It is a much better idea to keep them in a safe or at reception.

## DON'T TAKE PART IN PROMOTION EXCURSIONS

Unsuspecting tourists get taken in by people handing out flyers offering free tours of the island along with coffee and cake. The gullible are then coerced into buying what are often shoddy articles such as thermal blankets at exorbitant prices. Don't take part in these trips – there is no such thing as a free lunch!

## DON'T BE RIPPED OFF IN RESTAURANTS

Bread is a part of every Spanish meal and it used to be free. Today, it is served without being ordered … and later turns up on the bill. As a rule: if you have reason for not being satisfied, ask for the *hojas de reclamación* (complaints forms) that every restaurant is required to have and which are controlled by the state. That is the way to make your criticism known.